One Life Is Not Enough

One Life
Is Not
Enough

My Life in Russia
and the Broadway and
Hollywood Years

Barbara Barondess MacLean

HIPPOCRENE BOOKS
New York

For information, address: Hippocrene Books, Inc.
171 Madison Avenue, New York, NY 10016.

Library of Congress Cataloging-in-Publication Data

MacLean, Barbara Barondess.
   One life is not enough.

   1. MacLean, Barbara Barondess.   2. Moving-picture
actors and actresses—United States—Biography.
I. Title.
PN2287.M184A3   1986   791.43'028'0924   [B]   86-19536
ISBN 0-87052-338-4

Printed in the United States of America.

Contents

Acknowledgments

THIS book owes its existence to an evening I spent at Horace Liveright's house. That night I met the three giants he was publishing: Eugene O'Neill, Sinclair Lewis, and Theodore Dreiser. They were fascinated with the story of my family's escape from Russia, and persuaded Horace to offer me an advance to write it, but I rejected the offer because I felt then that my life was largely before me, and I intended to pursue a life worth writing about.

That was 1928. Since then I've done a lot of living, and I've had a lot of encouragement from other famous writers I respect and admire—from S. N. Behrman, Sidney Sheldon, Alvin Moscow, Sheila Graham, Robert Winter-Berger, Edwin Kennebeck, and my editor at Hippocrene, Jack Steinberg. Encouraging also have been the media, who have been wonderful to me since 1926; my family and loving friends who read the early drafts, my devoted secretary, Eileen Madison, and Alan Freed, who typed and retyped the endless rewrites and revisions; my wonderful agent, Bertha Klausner, whose encouragement and effort were most important; and my father and mother, wherever they are.

To all, I dedicated my story, now 58 years later, with the hope that it will inspire the young and old not to give up their dreams and desires—to keep going and learning, and trying to find the work they love. Life is a one-way ride and must be enjoyed every day. It is the ride, not the destination, that's the challenge, the happiness of pursuit, not the pursuit of happiness.

Foreword
A Baggage of Memories

GEORGE GERSHWIN'S *Porgy and Bess* opened at the Metropolitan Opera in February 1985, fifty years after its original production on Broadway. It opened up a whole bag of memories that we carry with us like baggage all our lives, often remembering moments of bygone years as if they had just happened. The last time I saw George was in Beverly Hills, California, in 1938, in a nightclub called Mocambo. I had not seen him since 1932, and it was a happy moment for me to introduce him to my husband, Douglas MacLean. It was only a few months after that George died, and I will always remember his compliment on the night we met. *Porgy and Bess* was opening in Los Angeles that first week we met, and I mentioned that Douglas and I would be at the opening. He said: "Please call me and let me know what you think of it." My answer was an astonished: "George! You want to know what *I* think of it? I have the records. It's beautiful!" He was so pleased, and I was so proud.

I first met George at a party in 1926 at the Stronskys (a noted medical family) on Fire Island. I liked him immensely. I had been an "instant celebrity" for only a couple of months, although I was beginning to get attention from "older" men in their twenties. I viewed them from the perspective of a girl still in her teens. I learned then that being a well-known young beauty has advantages and disadvantages. And the disadvantages loomed large and unattractive. I just didn't want to be mauled by every Tom, Dick and Harry. To begin with, I became very choosy about whom I made dates with. Actually, the first dates I had were with newspapermen and columnists, with whom I felt safe, particularly when I learned very fast that I had an unusual value to them. They found the tales of my childhood and escape from Russia fascinating. I learned then that no matter what I did I was copy. When George and I first talked on the beach at Fire Island, I knew who *he* was, and although he had no idea of who I was, he found out in a few minutes. He seemed shy and asked me for my phone number. A week later he asked me to meet him where his music was being played and where he was to appear as the piano soloist. I had never heard Paul Whiteman's orchestra and had no idea what was going to be played.

I met him an hour before the scheduled concert and he took me to my seat. The auditorium was empty, and there I sat and waited, watching it fill with people and come alive. Then the orchestra started to tune up, the lights went off, and the concert began. When George came on stage and sat down at the piano to play *Rhapsody in Blue*, the ovation was stupendous. After the concert, I sat spellbound watching the people file out. He was *my* date! I couldn't believe it!

I enjoyed the many times I spent in his penthouse on Riverside Drive with people like Vladimir Dukelsky, whose name you'll recognize as Vernon Duke, Oscar Levant, Gus Kahn, J. P. McEvoy and many other great talents of the time. For me, it was heaven to sit on his terrace and listen while he was composing some of his immortal tunes. He was a very talented painter, too. I was flattered when he asked me to go with him to parties, after the first date.

I was present through most of the composing of *Showgirl* with

Gus Kahn, and perhaps that's why George took me to the opening night in 1929. That memorable night, I sat between him and Al Jolson. Jolson was in love with Ruby Keeler. It was her first Broadway show. Her coach was the famous Bill Robinson. She did a very intricate number, dancing down a flight of stairs. She was supposed to be singing at the same time, but she suddenly stopped. It wasn't ten seconds before Jolson stood up. The orchestra leader saw him and Jolson went into the song, "Liza," singing it to her right from the audience. By the time he finished one chorus, she had regained her composure and the audience went wild. (This incident was shown in the film, *The Al Jolson Story*, and it took me right back to my seat next to Gershwin.)

I have many wonderful memories of George in the short period of three years that I saw quite a bit of him. It was a warm, platonic friendship. We talked about art, our respective romances, everything. When George heard about my background and childhood, he was surprised and frankly astonished that I spoke English so well. I discovered that intelligent, talented and sensitive men who were attracted to me could be kept as friends and were willing to give me the respect and consideration that I gave them. I let them know that I demanded nothing but their friendship if they were willing to give it, but I was not ready for any possessive relationships . . . and it worked, sometimes. Also, in retrospect, I can see what can happen when a young man meets a girl who looks perfectly normal, American-as-apple-pie, sheltered, only to discover that she's been to Russia and back with twelve years of hell in between—bilingual, bright, ambitious, willing to work, fearless, and Miss Greater New York to boot! They were fascinated and attracted.

As I dig into my memories I find it wasn't always easy. I had a lot of disappointments, three and a half marriages and four careers. Some of these events were tragic, some were painful, and some just disappointing. As I write this—facing almost fourscore—I am so full of projects and plans that I can't help wondering how I'm going to get enough time to get it all done and pass on my experiences and the things I learned to young people who reach the crossroad decisions. I have few regrets, even with all the hits, runs and errors. The errors made me a happy and healthy survivor and taught me judgment. I've also learned that you can't fight events that happen when you have no control over them, any more than I can change the color of my eyes. Some people may think me a Pollyanna—but I'm not. I'm a realist, and when I look at my contemporaries who became the great stars of Broadway and the Superstars in the Shangri-la called Hollywood, I am very happy with my lot—as founder and president of the Barbara Barondess Theatre Lab, back and involved with the professional theatre, writing this book, three more in the oven, and all my other ambitious plans—all those books I hope to read, all the pictures I hope to paint, and all the people I hope to help. But I mustn't run ahead of myself. I hope you'll enjoy reading this book as much as I did writing it.

CHAPTER ONE

World War

July Fourth means many things to Americans: liberty, vacations, fireworks, summer fun. . . . To me it means a great deal more; by the grace of God it was the day I was born. If I had come into the world six months later, I probably wouldn't be here to tell the story.

My mother, Stella Barondess, who recalled very few details and couldn't tell you what she ate for breakfast, remembered every fact about my birth and often repeated it. I was born ten minutes after midnight in a caul—a membrane that sometimes covers the head of an infant at birth and, according to legend, is a lucky omen. My mother later insisted that my eyes were as blue as cornflowers and that I was an exceptionally even-tempered, angelic baby. I was named Mary; the Barbara came later. I think of my birthday as the greatest fortune because I was born on American soil, in Brooklyn.

Louis and Rose Sirkis, my mother's parents, came to America in 1902 with their five children. Mother, almost 17, was the oldest; Robert, 2, was the youngest. Grandfather was a Hebrew teacher and scholar, and acquired a few private pupils in Brooklyn. They were not Orthodox, and did not observe the kosher dietary laws, but they did attend the synagogue on the high holidays. It was grandma who brought me into the world. Grandmother gave me the first slap to make me breathe, and I was frightened of her as long as she lived. It was she who filled out my birth certificate—a piece of paper that was to play a most important part in my life and in my parents' lives.

Of course my grandparents in Russia were delighted to learn that they had a grandchild. They wrote back that they were yearning to see the new family and kept up their campaign to bring us back to Russia. They sent money and pointed out to Father that he could always return to America after a few weeks or months if he wanted to. Father resisted their urgings for a short while, sure that with his intelligence and diligence he would soon be able to earn a good living with a publishing house. Besides, he thought the baby was too young for such a long voyage.

My father, Benjamin Barondess, was a handsome man with brown hair, light skin and brilliant violet eyes, and I inherited his coloring. He was gentle and quiet. The story of how he came to America in 1906, met Mother, fell in love with her and the United States and decided to settle down was a romantic tale. He was born on the border of the Ukraine January 17, 1880. After he graduated from the University of Kiev his parents sent him on a trip around the world. He was twenty-six years old, and that was a good way to avoid service in the Russian army.

He arrived in New York after Siberia and the Orient, on his way back to Europe, when a Russian friend introduced him to an eighteen-year-old Russian girl, Stella Sirkis, in Stuyvesant Park in New York City. Mother had golden blonde hair, cream color skin and grey eyes. She was vivacious and impulsive. It was love at first sight, and they were married six weeks later.

The young couple found an apartment in Brooklyn, and Benjamin took a job in Manhattan's garment district to see them through while he went to night school to learn English. In a couple of months he spoke it better than Stella, whose family had brought her here four years before. Benjamin was a linguist, spoke German and French and had traveled in Europe.

It isn't hard to imagine the concern his parents felt when he wrote them about his sudden marriage. Benjamin's father was a prosperous Ukrainian "Lumber King." His parents, naturally alarmed, started a campaign to lure him back to the home country, in which they were aided by my mother, for she had had enough of frugal living in genteel near-poverty. Her family came from the province of Podolsk, near the Polish border. Her middle-aged parents brought her here with two sisters and two brothers. When Father described his family's townhouse in Kiev, and their country house among the great fruit orchards of nearby Zhitomir, his father's lucrative business, and the carriage and servants, she begged him more and more fervently to take her back to meet them.

Father couldn't ignore her pleas entirely, because suddenly there was a depression in America in 1907, and he was not making much money. But he soon had a strong argument in favor of staying put: Stella was pregnant.

As I have already mentioned, my grandparents in Russia were delighted to learn that they were to have a grandchild. Stella added her urging to his parents' and by the time I was five months old, he gave in to the pressure. He was happy at last to see her so jubilant as they prepared for the hard and tedious trip in the middle of winter.

I was too young to remember anything about that journey, and I have forgotten most of what Father and Mother told me about it, but I know that my grandparents received us with open arms, enchanted with the new grandchild. I was six months old when we arrived in Russia in January 1908.

Father was one of seven children. His older sister, Aida, was a doctor of medicine—an unusual profession for a woman in those days in Russia. Father was the oldest of four boys. His brothers were Ovcei, Abraham, Volodya Lenya; his younger sister was Fanya.

Mother's beauty, enthusiasm, and childlike charm completely won the family. She felt like Cinderella as they showered her with luxuries. She had her first fur coat, servants, and beautiful clothes. Grandmother was wonderful to her. She was back in her native land, where she did not have to struggle with the English language. It was the easy life she dreamed about but never hoped to have.

Mother saw no reason to return to the United States. She had never experienced such luxury. Once she had tasted the life of ballet and opera with my grandparents in Kiev and the comfortable country life in Zhitomir, the prospect of struggling with Father in Brooklyn didn't tempt her to go back. She used her beauty and feminine instinct and ingratiated herself with my grandparents to keep us in Russia. Grandmother persuaded Grandfather to build us a special house with American conveniences.

Father didn't like arguments; he wanted my mother to be happy. And it is often easier to postpone decisions than to make them. He found the years slipping by and his plans for an exciting life in America growing dim. And so I grew up as a part of this exuberant family. It was a rich and peaceful life—for my first seven years.

Aunt Aida married another doctor, Alexey. They had one son, Volodya, my oldest cousin. Uncle Abraham was the handsome rebel of the family. Instead of working in my grandfather's lumber business, he wanted to be an artist, but settled for photography, which was lucky for me, because he took the photographs that now help revive the memories I am writing about.

Ovcei, my first uncle, who was next to my father, married the town belle, Tanya. The gossip was that she had been in love with my father, but after his marriage, she married his brother, who had always been in love with her. Ovcei was blond, blue-eyed and very serious. They had two children, a girl and a boy. Lenya, my third uncle, the youngest of the brothers, was studying dentistry. He had a thin, esthetic face, ash blond hair, and blue eyes. He was shy, and so was my youngest aunt, Fanya, who was very pretty. They were a handsome family except for the oldest sister, Aida, the physician, who was stocky with heavy features. She looked like my uncle Abraham, who was handsome, but she was not a pretty woman. She had the square face of Grandfather, who had a shock of grey hair and a beard. Grandmother was a fair, sweet, and gentle woman with blue eyes in an oval face. My father inherited her looks. Her parents were Greek Orthodox and her sister was a baroness.

I never heard any reference to religion, Christian or Jewish, and never heard any language but Russian, German, and French until I learned the meaning of the word "pogrom" and was told that we came from a prominent Jewish family whose roots were traced to Czechoslovakia and a town called Brandyc, very near Prague, in 1500. Nobody in the family practiced any rituals of the Jewish religion or dietary laws, but they all believed there was a God, and my father's philosophy was that there was one God for everybody and the ritual should be left to the individual to observe when he became of age. It was during the Russian Revolution that I learned about hate, bigotry, and the cruelty of man to man under the guise of religion. Justice Louis D. Brandeis, whose family origin is the same as mine, was brought up in the same way, I have been told.

No matter what my grandparents did to bribe my father with luxuries to make him stay in Russia, his dream was to return to America. Whatever Father told them about things he had seen in the United States, they tried to create and duplicate. The house they built for us in Zhitomir was red brick, had a flat roof, the first in Russia. The first floor had a large, magnificent parlor with French furniture, a dining room, library, sitting room, an enormous kitchen and a few rooms for help—the second floor had three master bedrooms and three small rooms—vast cellars and electricity with pushbutton switches, the first I had ever seen. All these ideas came from my father's glowing description of the kind of house we were going to have in America someday. The house was set off the road on about 5,000 acres of land. There was a beautiful lake and what seemed to me like miles of fruit orchards.

We had three cottages. Grandfather built one of them for a faithful old Polish man who had worked for the family in the lumberyards all his life. The other two were for the servants' families and farmers who took care of the land. All had large cellars that were used to store the jams and jellies, wine and brandied cherries, large barrels of sauerkraut with green apples put in to sour. The only comfort we didn't have were bathrooms with running water. We had a neat array of outhouses in a secluded part of the garden, about fifty feet from the house, and water for washing was brought in pitchers and buckets from the kitchen. In winter there were chamber pots.

I couldn't have been more than four or five, but I remember the Russian Easter ceremonies in the village with the peasants in all their finery, looking like the entire Moiseyev ballet. The Ukrainian peasant costumes were extraordinarily beautiful. The girls wore coronets of flowers woven of blue cornflowers and black-eyed susans in their long thick braids, with multicolored ribbon streamers hanging down in back. Their shirtwaists were made of natural linen embroidered in brilliant colors; their aprons colorful with embroidery and ribbons. The girls and boys always seemed happy, singing and dancing to the Russian-Ukrainian folk music.

The Friday ritual baking of bread is another rich memory. I loved to sneak into the kitchen and see the loaves of rye bread come out of the oven. Our cook, Olga, would save the largest bursting knuckle for me. I still can't pass a bakery and see a rye loaf with a burst knuckle without tasting the flavor of the hot bread with grilled white pork rubbed with garlic and salt. In the winter Olga would let me climb up to her winter bed, called a "petcha." It was an adobe shelf on the top of the baking stove and the warmest and most wonderful corner to hide in on a cold winter's night. On Saturday nights, during the winter, there was a lot of excitement when we took our baths in the middle of the kitchen amid boiling kettles of water, soap and towels.

The town was named Zhitomir, which means "a measure of rye." It had a population of about four thousand people, and was the chief city of the province of Valhynia. Surrounded by rich rye fields, meadowlands and forests, the town had one main street which led from the railroad station to the middle of town where my future school stood. Zhitomir couldn't have been more than a hundred miles from Kiev.

We stayed in the town fall, winter and spring. The summers we spent in our country house, or "dacha," on the edge of one of Grandfather's enormous woods, with a river in the back. Grandfather built these small dachas for all his children. On river-side we had curious bathhouses built on stilts over the water; they had, literally, four walls and a roof, with a bench around the sides. The floor was water. It was like having a permanent umbrella large enough to undress in, and was called the "banya." We would undress in the banya, leave our clothes on the bench and dive into the river nude. I don't remember ever seeing a bathing suit.

The summers were gorgeous. The front porch of the house faced right into the woods and nestled among the great trees. We picnicked in the woods, fished for crayfish, which in Russian we called "rack," from the sweet-water lake, and competed in picking wild strawberries, blueberries, blackberries, and raspberries. These expeditions were wonderful. We filled our baskets and our stomachs, chattering and giggling. When the baskets could hold no more, we would line our skirts with leaves to hold more of the berries. By the time we came home, we were exhausted, full of the flavor and odor of wild berries that were pungent and ripe and unlike any others I have tasted since. Every time I go to Paris and look at a basket of *fraises de bois*, for a moment I recapture the taste of those berries, but it can never be quite the same.

I had a private tutor and was studying French, German and the basic rudiments for entering Marinskya Gymnasia, which was a six-year classical school. After that, one went to the polytechnic schools for four years before one was eligible for the university. Our family was very conscious of education, an intellectual bunch. My tutor didn't have much patience with me or my aptitude as a pupil when it came to languages. Everybody knew that I was that oddity born in a far-off magic land. The tutor used to say, "You are so abominably bad and lazy when it comes to your French and German lessons, if you ever go back to your mother-country you'll have a terrible time learning the language." Otherwise, I was an excellent student, particularly in arithmetic. A fast one at any rate; I passed my examination sufficiently high in the other subjects to enter the very fine Marinskya Gymnasia.

The summer of 1914, before I began classes there, we came back from the dacha as usual in early September. On one of those magnificent, golden days, I went off to my favorite field to pick cornflowers and make a coronet and dream. My sister Rosalie had been born the October before—she became the star attraction—I was demoted, but it gave me more freedom to go off by myself. The air was velvet and the sun golden. The fields too were golden, and the wheat and rye were ripe and ready for harvesting. I used to love to go to the edge of the fields and look at the miles of wheat—like a sea of gold. The slightest breeze made them shimmer and wave, and they were almost taller than I was. The violet-blue cornflowers were nestled all around for miles. After picking the cornflowers my face was hot and my arms were filled. I stopped near a row of trees that separated the fields from the road, and lay down in the grass near a tree. It felt so cool against my flushed face. I looked at the blue sky filtered through leaves of the trees, with the pungent odors of flowers and the ripe wheat.

But even as I sat in the shade and wove my coronet, on that golden morning, I felt strangely restless. I tried to imagine the country I came from, and wondered if and when we would go back. Once two women had looked at me and whispered, "Malenkaya Americanka." When I asked my mother what they meant, she explained that I came from a land that was as remote as the moon, and that it was not an insult, it was a blessing. When would I be big enough to see that land? I was torn between my love of the beauty and familiar comforts around me and the tremendous aloneness that I felt because I felt alien. I belonged somewhere else.

When I finished the coronet and put it on my head, I scooped the rest of the flowers into my skirt and regretfully started for home. On my way, I saw some men pasting up signs on the wooden fences along the road. They were enormous posters, and across them in red letters was one word. It was a new word that I had never heard before, and, somehow, without knowing why, I sensed that it had an unpleasant element. I wanted to get home as fast as I could. When I asked Mother what it meant, her explanation was not very clear. It was almost two years later that I understood the real significance of the word "Voina" (War) and that Germany was the "enemy." For the next couple of years, the free and easy feeling seemed to be disappearing. The children were kept in ignorance, but we did notice that every once in a while a young man of one of the neighboring families would go away.

My best friend and playmate was Marina, whose mother died when she was a baby. Her older brother was studying medicine at the University of Kiev, and she lived with her father alone on the big estate next to us. She spent a lot of time at our home, which was always full of children—family and servants. We loved to be taken to the enchanting park near the school, which had the most beautiful ice-cream parlor I ever saw. Its garden was on the edge of a park, among trees under the open sky, surrounded by tall columns topped by giant mirrored finials. There were little round tables with marble tops among the tall lacy trees. The greatest treat was to be taken there in the early evening, when kerosene lamps on the tables threw a dancing, flickering light that reflected like a kaleidoscope on the silver finials. It was like a fairyland.

Another playmate was my cousin Volodya, whose parents

were both doctors, one of the handsomest boys around. He had dark brown hair, and velvet-brown eyes. He lived in another small town, Berdichev, about 25 miles away, but during the summer he would come to visit and stay at their dacha next to us. It was fun having him around. One afternoon in the late summer, when we were ten, we were all picking cherries, and Volodya and I were competing. I was reaching for the highest branch, but he grabbed my leg to keep me from getting there before him. I lost my balance and fell, with the cherries spilling out of my apron. As I toppled, he fell and grabbed a branch, but lost his footing and came down on top of me. I felt more shock than pain as I hit the ground, but Volodya was so frightened that his enormous eyes looked like those of a frightened doe.

Suddenly I began to feel a strange new consciousness. I felt wonderful, uncomfortable, and embarrassed all at the same time. My right leg ached a little and I couldn't move it but that wasn't important. In that fleeting moment, as he moved to lift himself up, I felt a good kind of pain, and wanted to put my arms around him, but we both blushed; he got up and ran for help.

After that, Volodya seemed something more than playmate, but I couldn't define what it was. I had a terrible crush. He was so serious, and suddenly remote, that I don't think his feeling for me was the same as mine.

One day, in 1916, when he and Marina and I were playing on the terrace of our house—suddenly there was a noise and everybody began running into the street. We were startled to see a procession of ragged, dirty men, some without shoes, some with perspiration streaming down their faces, caked with blood, with tattered clothes and parched lips, chained together like animals, clanking the chains as they dragged their sore and weary feet. Soldiers were driving, pushing and hitting them. I have never seen such cruelty. We couldn't believe our eyes; they looked hungry, thirsty, sick, and so young.

Within a few seconds I took command and issued orders—everybody followed. We ran to the houses, filled pails with water, and with all the food we could get our hands on stood by the road trying to hand them a drink of water or a piece of food. They grabbed at the fruit and bread like animals. The guards and soldiers tried to stop us, but we outnumbered them and we managed to get through to a few of the unfortunate souls. I couldn't understand why the guards were so cruel and what those men had done. The violence shook us, and when Mother tried to explain to me that the men were German prisoners, I was appalled. I couldn't understand why people had to be that cruel to each other.

I think it was that experience that made me buckle down to my studies. I became, from a fast but lazy student, a committed, dedicated and serious one. I started to read and I devoured books.

Father was very pleased. Mother couldn't have cared less; she was not interested in anything but her own comfort and appearance. The men in the family liked her flirtatious, feminine, friendly personality, but women did not. They were jealous of her good looks, but what anybody thought didn't concern her. She had a temper and managed to get almost everything she wanted from Father. If he didn't give in fast enough, she went over his head to my grandmother, who was diplomatic, gentle and kind. On several occasions I overheard Grandmother admonish my Aunt Tanya for being so hard on Stella. I heard Tanya say that Mother had no table manners. Father, on the other hand, never criticized her. He would explain to her in a very gentle way and sometimes he made me the example. I remember one incident, when I picked up a piece of chicken with my hands, my father said, "That's what the fork is for." In my smart-aleck mood, I answered, "Papa, fingers were made before forks." "Yes, you are perfectly right," he said, "but not yours."

But a wonderful new world opened for me, the world of books. I read every translation from the English into the Russian that I could, even to the Sherlock Holmes and Nick Carter mysteries that Father brought me. The little I knew about the

United States from what my parents told me became magnified in my young mind. The mechanical things, like the elevated trains that sounded like magic roller coasters, the mystery of the automat which took nickels in slots and gave out food, the tall buildings with flat roofs became my enchanted world and I couldn't wait to grow up and go back. Whenever I threatened to displease my mother by staying up half the night reading a book or refusing to eat, my mother bribed me with stories of my birthplace.

Another influence on my book reading was my cousin Volodya, who was with Marina and me one early evening on the porch when we saw a drunk leaning against the gate. Marina and I went over to him and saw, to our horror, that he was exposing himself. We ran back, and Volodya, seeing our alarm, went over to the man, spoke to him harshly and drove him away. Then Volodya came to us on the porch, laughing, and said, "You girls don't know much about men, do you? Why don't you go to the library in Marina's house and look at some of the medical books her brother brought from school?"

Later, we followed his advice and absorbed a lot of information, a bit precociously. Marina's father had quite a library. Besides the medical books, her brother had added books on history, and we also read Tolstoy, Pushkin, Dostoyevsky, and discovered with delight Guy de Maupassant. We thought we were so wise and sophisticated.

I had a deep voice, and my mother commanded me to eat raw eggs to make it higher. She was afraid I would grow up with a foghorn, and she used to tell me that it wouldn't be ladylike to have such a deep voice. I battled and cried, but I ate the eggs. They didn't change the timbre of my voice, however, and ten years later, it became a distinctive asset.

The next two years were a nightmare, and worse was yet to come. January 1, 1917, Rasputin was dead. We heard snatches of horrible atrocities and stories, but at the beginning we ourselves saw very little of this. March 1917—the Tsar and his family were imprisoned, it was whispered, and two factions were fighting over the future of Russia—Civil War! Pogroms were everywhere. Our families lived in dread. I was going to school sporadically; and we children were not allowed much freedom. A foreboding of disaster was everywhere. I would find Mother crying, blaming herself for keeping Father from going back to America. Now, she realized, it was no longer possible to leave Russia easily.

Our schooling became more and more erratic. We would go for a few days and then be kept home for a few days. Marina and I both went to the same school, and on the days when we did go, after classes were over at three o'clock, we would line up downstairs and wait for the teacher to dismiss us. Marina and I became inseparable.

One chilly spring day we put on our hats and coats to go home from school, but were ordered by our teacher to come back to the classroom. We were to do our homework and stay in the classroom until they dismissed us. We had never waited more than fifteen minutes before, so when this got to be longer than an hour, with no explanation from the teacher except that there was shooting and danger outside, I felt very uneasy. Rosalie, four years old, had been brought to school that day to stay with me for a short while, while Lena, our governess, went on an important errand. She was to come back to get us. My mother had gone to the country dacha to get it in order for the summer.

A long interval passed and still no Lena. Marina was a little heavier and taller than I, and looked older, but I was the leader and passed her a note to tell her that I was going to ask to go to the lavatory and she was to follow my lead a few minutes later. She took my suggestion. We had to leave our coats in the schoolroom, but by now we had no thought of the chilly air outside. I took Rosalie to the lavatory. While I waited for Marina, I climbed on top of wastebaskets, which I had put one on top of the other, upside down, and opened the window for Marina to follow me out. The school-yard was empty; even the gate man had taken shelter. I climbed out the window; Marina handed Rosalie to me and followed us out. Suddenly, we looked at each other. There wasn't a soul in the street. The silence was strange and ominous. It was like a dead city, evacuated. We heard a strange swish through the air, following a shot. It sounded like a firecracker or explosion. I was terrified, and Marina dug her nails into my arm. Poor Rosalie clung to me too.

I suddenly felt guilty. It had been my idea to make them come with me, and now it was my duty to be brave. We didn't say a word. We just crept along the side of the buildings and ran when we saw a clearing. The distance to home couldn't have been more than ten city blocks, but those were the longest ten blocks—something Rosalie talks about to this day. It seemed an eternity before we reached our street. As we got to our corner, we saw a woman run across the street, scream, and fall face down. We stood there, helpless and terrified. A couple of doors down we saw one side of the building on fire and crumbling.

When we finally got to the house we found everyone at home safe, except for Mother, who was still in the country. Father, my youngest aunt, and, to my surprise, Lena. She was so relieved to see us. She had come to the school just after we left. She was a German girl whom we had come to love, who was part of the family and served us faithfully until the day we left. We will always be indebted to her for her sacrifices, and, wherever she is, we will always bless her. She grabbed my sister, hugging her with a sigh of relief. Mama didn't get back from the country until almost ten that night.

The massacres that went on and the fear and insecurity forced most of Marina's family servants to go back to their farms and homes, except for her governess. Marina spent a great many nights in our house because their servants had dwindled down to two, and her brother was also coming home from Kiev less frequently during this troubled time. Her father was away from home a lot, and when she did not stay over with us, I would stay at her house.

She and I were becoming more aware—well beyond our years. We were taking piano lessons, and she was very talented. I couldn't learn to play chopsticks, but nobody cared. It was something to do each day to keep us off the streets. All I wanted to do was read books and transport myself on the magic carpet to that wonderful country I came from. President Woodrow Wilson had declared neutrality at the beginning of the war, in 1914. But now America was in the war with us and World War I was on in full swing.

Somewhere in between, in bits and pieces, we learned about things besides war that went on in the outside world. Every Russian child sees ballet, so we saw it too. Uncle Abraham, the photographer, even took Marina and me to our first movie. Our piano teacher, who also taught singing, decided to put on a play with the talented pupils, and since I couldn't sing and didn't play the piano, she asked me to play the part of a little boy, which intrigued me tremendously. But my parents forbade it. It was too dangerous to go to the rehearsals held at the teacher's house across town. I was heartbroken, but no hysterics or begging could change my parents' minds. I decided that I hated them and was sure I didn't belong to them—they had found me somewhere and I was a foundling. All the other children of my age were in the play. I decided to take matters into my own hands. With Marina in on it, I pretended that I was spending the time at her house, but sneaked off to rehearsals. I had never lied to or disobeyed my parents before. Although by then we had a telephone, one of those lovely French ones, it was used only in an emergency, and so no one bothered to call Marina's home to speak with me, so I was safe. We had no trouble going to rehearsals and back.

The night of the dress rehearsal, my parents decided to reward me for being a good girl and take me to see it. My teacher had innocently asked them to come. This was a tough one, and I was trapped, but it didn't take me long to figure out that if I asked my parents to let me go earlier because I wanted to help Marina with her costume before the play started, they would never suspect. I think they felt a little sorry for me because they had refused to let me be in it, and since they didn't suspect the elaborate plot, they readily agreed. While they were visiting and talking with other parents outside the auditorium, I went back-stage, got into my costume, put on my makeup—and suddenly I was terrified of what I had done and was actually frozen with guilt. But then the curtain went up, and I found myself on stage. The anticipation was exciting and wonderful, but the actual performance was a strange mixture. Waiting for my cue, I was paralyzed with fear that I would forget my first lines. I was also sure that my voice would fail me but when I heard my cue, suddenly an invisible hand seemed to guide me and I became in that instant the little boy. I went through it in a kind of a trance, two people in one, and then it was over.

I prayed that my parents would forgive me. But my perform-ance didn't soften their hearts. On the way home there was an ominous silence. They didn't say a word. I had an empty, sick feeling at the pit of my stomach. I wished I hadn't done it. It was so disappointing, not to have them say *something!* I felt guilty and suddenly very lonely. When we got home, I was ordered to my room, and my father gave me the only spanking or thrashing I ever got. My bottom hurt; my pride was shattered. I had thought of myself as so grown up. My mother never said a word. That night my father brought me a board and some nails, and hung it in my room, commanding me to hammer a nail into it every time I did something wrong—and he said he would trust me and my conscience, and would explain the purpose of the board when it was full.

CHAPTER TWO

Violence, Hiding and Rape

DURING the following troubled months, I found more opportunity to be alone, except for the time I spent with Marina in school. No one paid much attention to us. Our parents spent more time huddled around the dining room table, drinking hot glasses of tea and talking about the war, the Tsar and the Revolution. The country was in a state of civil disaster. I was allowed occasionally to be seen but seldom, if ever, heard. My big thrill was to refill my father's glass. It was quite an operation. The huge silver samovar actually held only water, kept boiling hot by a central core of pipe that contained fiery coals. Underneath was a perforated plate through which air fanned the coals. A little pot at the top held the "essence" of the tea, a super strong brew. I enjoyed pouring a little of this essence into a glass, then filling the glass with hot water from the spigot.

The faces of the grownups became graver as they talked about the political problems which of course were not clear to me— probably not even to them. The words and terms were new, and everyone felt terrified and helpless. They talked about the assassination of Rasputin. I didn't know who he was, but I had heard the name all during my childhood, along with Bolshevik, Menshevik, Duma, Kerensky, Trotsky, Lenin. Later we heard that the Tsar, the Tsarina and all the princesses and the little Tsarevich were taken from Tsarskoye Selo. St. Petersburg, the capital of Russia, was renamed Petrograd. Chaos, civil war and brutality were raging around us. There were mysterious changes in government, and it seemed that every few weeks we had different rulers in our little town of Zhitomir. People talked in whispers, and the older students and young men met secretly. There were heated arguments about politics. Almost every week we heard that one of our friends' sons was killed or wounded in the war. My youngest uncle, Lenya, went into the army. Abraham was off to Petrograd on a mission for Grandfather. My grandmother became very ill. My Aunt Fanya's husband also left for the army. My father and his younger brother Ovcei were left to help Grandfather run his vast lumber business. We heard words like "capitalist" and "confiscation," and our carefree, happy, loving life was gone forever. Gone were the excursions, the picnics, the trips to ballet, opera, circus and even to our magical ice cream parlor near the park.

Now we were rarely taken out in the evening, and the occasional daytime trip was a tremendous treat. In earlier days, when my father would hand us a ruble and send us off, it would buy ice cream for at least ten of us. Then one day in 1917, as we were about to go there he handed me 250 rubles. I thought he had made a mistake, but he looked at me and said, "No, my child, I didn't make a mistake; it's only worth a ruble now." Some time later, in 1918, he gave me a note for 5,000 rubles—it was the last money produced in Tsarist Russia. The next note he handed me was in 1919 and that was for 10,000 rubles, which I didn't have a chance to use either. That was the first money produced under the new regime, and on each side of it was written a phrase in a different language, including English, "Workers of the World Unite." I have it framed to remind me of the three trips to the ice-cream parlor I never took. But I am running ahead.

In the summer of 1917, Marina was growing fast. She grew about four inches to my one and gained a lot of weight. I was small and scrawny for ten. I lost myself in reading everything I could get my hands on, and spent my spare hours alone at the edge of our lake, reading or watching toads and marine life. At night I waited until everyone was asleep, then put on my light. My room was next to my parents. They caught me more than once and turned the light out in the middle of the night, but no pleading or scolding on their part stopped me, until my eyes began to feel as if I had sand in them. Then they became inflamed and red-rimmed.

My mother was frantic and took me to a doctor, who prescribed glasses. Horrified, she told him that under no circumstances would she allow her daughter to wear glasses, so the doctor shrugged his shoulders and gave her an alternative remedy—a heavy paste, the consistency of beehive honey, which she was to apply to my eyes when I went to bed. It literally pasted my eyelashes together so I couldn't open my eyes until she rescued me in the morning by washing it off with warm water. I had no choice, and the dreaded fear of going blind forced me to obey.

This treatment lasted about ten days and, in those nights lying in bed with my eyes pasted together, I had an opportunity to reflect, plan, and dream. I could pretend that I was a pampered princess sleeping on her bed of perinas. A perina was a goose-down mattress, a most luxurious symbol of wealth. Of course, the more of them you slept on, the wealthier you were. The peasants slept on straw. I was miserably restless and complained that my bed was not soft enough. I claimed I could still feel the bed slats through my perina, so my mother kept piling them on until I had eight of them and was satisfied. That was heaven; when I lay on them I felt as if I were floating. My father laughingly named me the "princess and the pea." Just outside my window—what could be more Chekhovian?—was my own cherry tree. Grandfather customarily gave a cherry tree to every child, and when harvest time came, that tree was to be picked only by the child it was allotted to, and whatever friends he or she chose. My cousin Volodya and I loved to gather those sweet cherries.

Lena gave me her most prized possession, a lovely silver and enameled icon with a picture of the Virgin, to hang over my bed, to bless and heal my eyes.

As I have already indicated, I rarely heard any discussion about religion, except once when I overheard an argument between my father and mother. She was crying because he didn't want to go with her to the synagogue. I remember he told Mother that she could go if she wished, but he didn't feel the need—that he felt it was hypocritical to go on high holidays and ignore religion the rest of the year. He had his own method of praying and believing in God, he said. There was a scene and tears, and I was confused and curious.

When I asked for an explanation, my father told me that there was one God, but there were different ways of believing. He said he liked the way he was taught, that the way to serve God was to adhere to rules of decency and humanity. He said that all the things in the Bible, including the Old and New Testaments, were trying to arrive at the same conclusion and all I needed for my religion were the basic, simple rules—the first of the ten commandments, "Thou shalt have no other gods before me," and the Golden Rule of the New Testament. He taught me his favorite little prayer. It was the same prayer of Reinhold Niebuhr, "God grant me the serenity to accept the things I cannot change, the courage to change the things I can, and the wisdom to know the difference."

In the summer of 1917, Rosalie had the croup and I was sent to stay with Marina to avoid getting it. Marina had a cold. One night her father and brother, who was home from the University in Kiev, had gone to a meeting, and we were alone in the house. I was reading out loud to her when there was a knock at the

door. When I asked "Who's there?" a raucous male voice ordered
me to open the door. I asked him to please tell me what he
wanted. He answered that if I didn't open the door, he would
smash it down. I tried to explain that we were alone. I felt
terrified, not knowing what to do. I opened it. There, facing me,
stood three unshaven, filthy, slimy, enormous men, reeking of
liquor. They were not wearing regular soldiers' uniforms, but
they were in some kind of uniform I couldn't recognize. The
biggest one, who looked more like an ape than a man, shoved
me aside and walked into the living room where Marina was
lying on the couch in her night dress and robe, covered with
blankets. She was beautiful, with red hair and green eyes, and
looked older than her eleven years. The big one looked down at
her and lifted the blanket as he ordered one of the men to keep
watch outside, the other to find some vodka and hold me. He
looked at us with shifty, lecherous eyes. I stood in front of
Marina, pleading with them to leave. I felt so small and helpless
and terrified. I was just ten and I guess I looked about eight,
which was fortunate for me. They laughed in my face. Marina
was running a fever and my move to protect her seemed to
awaken a strange delight in this ape. He grabbed me, pushed
me aside, and sat down next to her. I said she was sick, and
begged him to leave her alone. He slapped me. Poor Marina
trembled, but didn't utter a sound.

The more I pleaded, the more annoyed he became. The other
two were ransacking the room for vodka. I was trapped and
didn't know what to do. I didn't know whether to try to run out
for help, or to help them get the vodka. I felt helpless and terror
stricken when I realized they wouldn't let me go. Marina started
to cry and I screamed. The ape clamped his filthy hand over my
mouth. The rancid smell of his breath and dirty clothes nause-
ated me. I suddenly became dizzy and broke into a cold sweat. I
couldn't breathe and felt faint. The other two found the vodka
and came back into the room with a bottle in each hand. The ape
literally tossed me to one of them and told him to keep me quiet.
The third one went on the lookout. I was dragged to another

room, but I heard Marina as the brute tore her nightgown—
heard her screams and stifled moans.

Suddenly we heard somebody approaching. The three
grabbed the bottles and ran out the back door. Marina's father
and brother came in to find us huddled together. I was sobbing
and trying to stop her hysteria. Her pathetic moaning is a sound
I shall never forget. The ape had broken her wrist and she was
bleeding and holding her hand between her legs. Time plays
strange tricks with memory. Even as I write about it now, it
seems impossible that I was there. The blessing of time makes
me remember it as if it were something I had dreamed of, or that
I had once seen in a movie.

Poor little Marina, a very sensitive girl, had a complete nervous breakdown. I wasn't told much about it. Later I was horrified to hear that she had died and everyone said that in her
case it was for the best. I was never told the details. I might have
been more distressed about her suffering, about losing my best
friend, if the fears and confusions and terrors of those days
hadn't distracted me. Or, maybe, since there was nothing I or
anyone could do for her, not thinking about it was my way of
surviving. But my board was getting filled up with more and
more nails. Why had I opened that door?

I stopped going to school, my father giving me lessons at home.
We lived in a constant state of suspense. My youngest aunt gave
birth to a little girl, but all our joys were now shadowed by fear.

"Pogrom" was another familiar word by now. I learned that the
guerillas who attacked and raped Marina belonged to a gang
headed by Ataman Petlura. He was one of the barbarian Cossacks who decided that all Bolsheviks were Jews, and so their
motto was "Kill the Jews and free Russia." And the Bolsheviks'
motto was "Kill the capitalists and free Russia." We were right in
the middle. Grandfather and Grandmother were in and out of
Kiev. Petlura was credited with most of the massacres in our
region. His men had a field day of pillaging, raping and killing.
They needed very little excuse. We lived in constant fear and

dread, because they always came back to Zhitomir to resupply themselves after ravaging the outlying villages. Petlura escaped to France in 1922, where he lived for a couple of years in luxury with the blood money he had amassed. Happily, he didn't enjoy it for long. A young Russian Jewish boy, by the name of Schwartz, whose family Petlura had murdered, killed him in Paris in 1927. Small revenge. Schwartz was tried but acquitted.

My Aunt Fanya's baby girl was three weeks old when we got word that we had to go into hiding—another impending massacre by Petlura's gang or some other band spawned by the political chaos. But now it was worse. Our houses were known, and we were running out of places where we could hide. Peasants and Grandfather's employees were our only chance, and the old faithful watchman, Illiya, for whom Grandfather had built a house on our property, came to our rescue. His cellar was large and warm. It had one entrance that could be boarded up and camouflaged. We had no choice; we accepted this haven gratefully. We didn't know how long we would have to stay there, but we prepared for two weeks. It was a low, adobe room with a concrete floor about 20 by 30 feet. One tiny window, very high, gave us a silver of light. No water, no lavatory, and no lights. There, amongst the sauerkraut barrels and jars of fruit, we settled in, on straw mattresses with blankets, kerosene lamps, candles, and non-perishable foods. We were boarded up in the cellar. Hooks were nailed to the other side of the new boards to make it look like a coat rack.

There were Mother, Father, Rosalie and I, my youngest aunt and her baby, Uncle Voloyd's new wife, Vera, my Uncle Ovcei, my Aunt Tanya, and their two children, Grandfather and Grandmother, who had been very ill and looked like a transparent ghost with her lovely white hair and beautiful face, always fastidious in her lace collars and brooch. Grandfather, whom I had always thought of as a virile, hot-tempered man with a roaring voice, his head held high with its wonderful streak of white hair, was drained and crushed by this experience. We all huddled in the dark, quiet cellar. We had two boxes and a board for a table. Mattresses and blankets on the floor were our beds. We knew Illiya was risking his life, and we felt buried alive. It was the end of October 1918.

After seventeen days, our food ran out. We had become accustomed to the meager fare, but this was devastating. The air was foul and rancid. My aunt had almost choked the baby trying to keep her from crying. By this time, my mother was having violent morning sickness, her nerves were at a breaking point, and she realized that she was pregnant.

Finally, my father and uncle couldn't stand it any longer. Grandfather insisted that he would get out and see what he could do, but his sons wouldn't hear of it. My father insisted that it was his duty as the oldest son. I begged to go with them— I was the oldest of the next generation. They refused absolutely.

It was agreed that my father would get out to see what he could do, appraise the situation on the outside, and, at least, bring us some fresh food, and, if Illiya opened the door, they would carry out the waste and let a little fresh air in to succor us. When it got dark, Illiya unboarded the wall and my father started up the stairs. Father didn't see me behind him, and the rest of the family was too involved in getting rid of the waste. When they discovered I'd escaped, they didn't dare raise their voices. I had been afraid that Father would discover I was following him, but in his haste, he didn't turn to look back, and I kept following at a safe distance.

I think he must have walked about five blocks toward the shopping district. Suddenly I saw silhouettes of two men dart out in front of him. I couldn't hear what they said, but I saw my father put his hands in his pockets. I crept nearer, holding my breath. I heard Father say, "But I've given you everything I have," when I saw one of the men whip out a shiny object and heard a familiar sound as I jumped like someone possessed and threw myself in front of my father, reaching my arms around his neck. As I did, I intercepted the second bullet, which hit my right shoulder. I think the shock of my jumping out of nowhere startled the men. Father and I fell to the ground and the men fled.

I didn't feel any pain initially, just a sting. Blood from Father's throat was coming through his shirt and collar and was all over me. He was unconscious. I felt an excruciating pain in my shoulder as I got up, but I stumbled and ran until I got to a door with a sign on it that said "Doctor." I rang the bell and blurted out my story. My dress was covered with blood. I fainted.

I was told later that my father would have bled to death in a few more minutes. Interesting how our minds photograph places and things, to be filed away in the subconscious for future use. I had never been to that particular doctor before, but I had remembered the sign on the house. I had passed it often before, and it had etched itself into my mind.

A few days later, when I regained consciousness, I was in my grandfather's house with my right arm and shoulder in a cast. The bandits had disappeared, and the family was back home. The first thing I asked was, "Where is Father?" He was alive, they told me, and had been taken to Petrograd by Aunt Tanya. My mother was too ill with nervous shock, and the family was afraid to let her accompany my father for fear of a miscarriage. If we had only waited in the basement just one more night, this might have been avoided.

Grandmother had her first heart attack, and the household was set up like a hospital. With Mother pregnant, and my right arm in a cast, we were a sorry lot. Tanya stayed with my father in Petrograd, and Fanya was busy with her baby. Our faithful Lena had her hands full. Grandfather and Uncle Ovcei were grim and plotting all the time—what, I didn't know then. They would go to the lumberyards and be away all day, sometimes not coming home until late at night, and we saw very little of them.

My father was being attended in the Petrograd hospital by one of the former Tsar's personal physicians. Both my grandfather and uncle had been to see him. They were trying to make a decision about an operation, something new that they were being advised about. Father had been shot right through the vocal cords, and there was only a slim chance that he would survive the operation. He was to have a tracheotomy which would enable him to breathe through a silver tube inserted into the newly created opening. He might eventually develop some kind of speech. Father decided to risk the operation.

The doctors, Aunt Aida and her husband, who lived in Berdichev, went to Petrograd to be with him, and my cousin Volodya came to stay with us. My mother insisted on going to Father and so she left and Tanya returned. Although I was happy to see Volodya again, I wanted to go with Mother, afraid that I would never see either of them again. But everyone explained that I must take care of Rosalie and the rest of the children; with my arm in a cast, I would only be an added burden. They assured me that everything would turn out all right and that my cast would have to be on my arm in order to keep the muscles from shrinking. I had been shot in a vulnerable joint in my shoulder. There was danger that my arm would not grow as I got older and be shorter than the other. So I had to stay behind. Mother promised to bring me a beautiful wristwatch from Petrograd.

The days stretched into weeks, and I felt frustrated and alone. I couldn't help anybody because the cast was heavy, and doing things with my left hand when I was righthanded was difficult— I felt useless. Even Volodya's serious, handsome face didn't cheer me up.

The mail was terribly irregular, and travel by train was increasingly dangerous. We knew that Uncle Lenya was at the front, but we didn't know where. One night the doorbell rang and he was brought in. He had been shot between the hip and the knee, and had been lying in some farmhouse for a week, delirious, while the daughter of the farmer, Maria, a lovely girl who had studied teaching and nursing, took care of him. When he was lucid enough to tell her his name and where he came from, she managed to put him in a wagon and bring him home.

When the doctor was summoned, he said that he was afraid gangrene was setting in.

I was elected to hold the kerosene lamp with my left hand that night while the wound was cleaned. I saw the doctor wrap an instrument the size of a long pencil and put it in the wound and pull it out the other side. He had no anesthesia. My uncle fainted with the pain. This process went on for a few days. Finally, they decided that the only way to save Lenya's life was to amputate his leg. My cousin Volodya and I held the lamps while Maria, who had stayed on to help take care of him, assisted the doctor in sawing off my uncle's leg. Volodya, who knew something about medicine, helped by holding Lenya steady with his other hand. I admired his ability to keep his self-control and do just what the doctor wanted. I closed my eyes, but I could hear my uncle's moans and smell the sickening odor. When they finished, I threw up. My uncle survived and married Maria.

CHAPTER THREE

Rough Going

W E RECEIVED word that Father had come through the operation all right and was on his way home with Mother. All of us went to the station and anxiously waited for the train to pull in. The snow was beautiful and the station very quiet. The usual activity of our railroad station had lessened considerably, because nobody traveled there unless someone who was wounded or ill had to be picked up. We heard the far-off sound of a whistle and saw the train like a fly on the horizon; we watched it become larger and larger as it came toward us.

As it pulled into the station and stopped, I scanned every door and window, wondering which way they would get off. Searching for the familiar faces, suddenly I saw Mother smiling and waving in a doorway, but I didn't see Father and I ran toward her as fast as I could, looking up, as she was stepping down, when suddenly somebody grabbed me and picked me up. Terrified, I looked into a strange bandaged face with a broken nose, and unshaven where the face wasn't bandaged. I let out a scream as the stranger hugged me; I looked into his blue eyes and realized that this was my father.

He didn't and couldn't say a word. Just kept hugging me until

41

my breath stopped, as tears streamed down his bandaged face. My handsome father had come back disfigured and wrapped in bandages. I started to sob with him when I realized he couldn't speak.

He wouldn't let go of me as we all piled into the sleighs to ride home on that memorable, brilliant, snow-white day. All the way home, I wondered how there could be so much pain and misery and cruelty in the light of such beauty. We were all laughing, crying, and singing as we rode home from the station, and everyone realized it was a miracle—deep down they had never believed that Father would make it.

We all settled down to make our adjustments—Lenya hobbling on his crutch, and my father with his pad and pencil, the only means of communicating with us. Whatever pain he suffered, he never let us know. It was about this time that Grandmother died. Grandfather never got over the loss, became a crushed, stooped, old man. I never got over not being allowed to go to her funeral because it was not safe. I saved the newspaper notice of her death, on the front page of the local paper, as if it proved that she was really dead. That was 1919, and I still have it.

After a while, Lenya moved into a little house of his own and started to practice dentistry, with his faithful Maria, who became his nurse, his wife and his strength.

The execution of the royal family shocked the world. The Bolsheviks were now in power, and Russia signed a treaty with Germany. America signed an armistice, but the Russian Civil War raged. Mother was expecting a baby in May. Father was crippled for life. My best friend was dead. The dream of going back to America was fast disappearing. With the country going through its bloodiest conflict in human history, the new regime in control of our city, we went back to live in our own house and walked the streets with less fear of being shot, for a little while. But we still were fearful because we were capitalists.

Most of Grandfather's land and possessions were confiscated.

Food was rationed. To have more than the barest amount of sugar and salt was considered a crime, but life went on. And on May 16, 1919, my sister Ann was born, and was nicknamed Nucy.

I was almost twelve, and my arm was healed except for the scar I still bear as a souvenir. Awful as life was, our friends were beginning to be hopeful and there was much talk about escaping to other parts of the world. I begged my father to tell me when we would finally go to America. He had developed a rasping hoarse whisper, difficult to hear and understand. He said he would let me know when the time came, and I waited. It was about the early fall of 1919 that my board attained its full quota of nails. I asked my father, "What now?" His answer was "Pull them all out," as he handed me the hammer. I did. "But what about the holes that are left?" I asked. "That's the rub," he answered. "The holes are always there."

It was Christmas, 1919. The family—consisting of Mother, Father, Grandfather, Uncle Ovcei, Aunt Tanya, Aunt Fanya, Uncle Lenya and his wife Maria, my Aunt Aida and her husband Alexey, and their son, Volodya, and I—were sitting around the dining table. The shining silver samovar and the glassware on the sideboard were my domain after dinner. Volodya and I were the only children present because we were over twelve. The conversation turned, as usual, to the people who had been able to escape. My father was sitting with the pad and pencil that he used for communication when there were many people present, instead of attempting to speak. Suddenly, he picked up his pencil and started to write. I was his messenger; he handed me the note, and I took it to my mother. She looked at the paper with wild joy and said, "The time has come—we are leaving for America in the next two weeks."

Suddenly the room was a bedlam of joy, laughter and tears and chatter about the route, the money, the jewelry. How would we get out? How much cash could we get together? The rubles were worthless; gold coins and diamonds were the only things that would get us out. We had a long journey ahead. Once my father made up his mind, we never looked back. He never wavered.

During the next two weeks we packed all the warm clothes we could take. We were sworn to secrecy. Carefully and methodically our plans were made. Everyone volunteered to help and everyone in the family gave up the gold in their possession. My father signed over all his interest in the business, in the house and property to his family. Emotions were mixed. We were going home, and for us there was hope. The rest of them were trapped. A couple of days before we left, Father called a conference. He explained—writing in the pad, trying to whisper in his toneless voice—that we were forced to take very little with us. As far as possessions were concerned, I would have to choose my few allotted souvenirs with care because I would have to carry them and care for them. The choice was not easy. I finally chose Grandmother's emerald earrings, my icon, the six silver knives and one mangled one, the family pictures, the newspaper notice of Grandma's death, my grandmother's black lace shawl, my small black challis shawl, and, last but not least, my ermine coat. My father's American friend had sent him an American dictionary in 1917; it was the only possession he took. How fortunate I am to be a saver. Somewhere in the back of my mind I must have been aware that I would need proof when my story was written, otherwise no one would believe it. I have seen expressions of doubt on so many faces when I mention my experiences. The expression seems to me, "Really? A likely story!"

Three weeks later, on the Russian New Year's Eve, at one o'clock in the morning, we quietly left the house by climbing through the window of my room into the garden, past my favorite cherry tree. We walked the short distance to the end of the orchard, and there was a hay wagon provided by an old driver. Our faithful Lena and her boyfriend, Petrook, were throwing a party for the local Bolshevik sentries, getting them drunk in our large cellar on our vodka and cherry brandy. I took a long last look at my room, the bed in which I had pretended to be a princess and sneaked in so many books to read. The cherry tree was asleep for the winter; its bare branches were covered with a cold mantle of pure, glistening snow. I would never see the tree again, would never watch it bloom with its fragrant, white blossoms, never again pick the cherries with my cousin Volodya. Never again would I help to pick the vegetables. I remembered the taste of luscious ripe tomatoes and cucumbers. My heart was heavy. Suddenly all the sad experiences in memory vanished, and I was conscious of only one face—Volodya. We were leaving home, friends and our family.

I would never see him again!

In the belt of my panties were sewn my grandmother's emerald earrings. She had willed them to me. Mother, eight-month-old Nucy, Rosalie, who was six, and I climbed into the wagon first; my father followed. Then we sank deep into the hay with our few bags of possessions, to ride away from the horror and nightmare forever we thought.

We traveled all night. Our clothes were warm. We were covered with the hay, but our breath froze in the cold winter night and I kept thinking about my room, my sanctuary. Every inch of it was photographed in my mind so accurately that I can close my eyes and see it to this very day.

The moon was bright, and the night clear and cold. The snow was so brilliant with the reflection of the moon that one could almost read by it. We huddled together under the hay. The crunch of snow under the wheels was the only sound except for my mother's voice as she whispered over and over to the baby, cradled in her arms, "In the good and blessed hour, in the good and blessed hour, in the good and blessed hour." Then there was silence, and suddenly I woke at our first stop. It was just before daybreak. We were to sleep hidden in the barn of a small farm until nightfall when the next hay wagon would take us to the next stop.

For two weeks we traveled at night, arriving at farmhouses at dawn. It was all prearranged; we would be hidden in barns, where we were fed and would sleep. At times a farmer would have courage enough to sneak us into the farmhouse so we could get next to the fire and perhaps Mother could wash the baby.

Everything went relatively smoothly until we reached our last stop on Russian soil, the tiny village of Ostrog, at what was then the border of Poland. It had been prearranged for a school teacher to hide us in a small house for a few days while we planned our strategy for crossing the border. When we arrived, the frightened teacher, a spinster, white as a sheet, greeted us with the news that our escape was known. My father's and mother's pictures were posted at the railroad station and every public edifice. We were to be brought back.

Father decided there was no turning back. We would stay under cover for a few days, and somehow we were going to get across the border. "Hang on, Stella," Father would say to Mother. "We'll get there." We never left the room we were in. We couldn't walk out in the street even to see what the town looked like.

After a few days of hiding, my father devised a plan. We would cross separately into Poland—Mother, Rosalie, and Nucy in one wagon, then Father and I, because I could speak for him. We were used to his horrible whisper, but he was not easily understood by strangers. The border town on the Polish side was Kovno. There was a greater chance of Mother's getting across with two small children, so Father and I would go first, and if we got across that would make it still easier for her. The money was divided, and Father's and my share went into the money-belt around my waist. Mother had her fur coat and her jewels. With tearful goodbyes, Father and I left in the middle of the night.

Whatever philosophy I have today I think was formed in the days that he and I spent together. My little prayer was enriched by the addition of the 23rd Psalm, and we kept repeating it until I could say it in my sleep. Now that I look back, I wonder how Father had that tremendous courage and compassion. As we rode in the hay wagon I bargained with God that if we got across the border, I would never do anything to make Father ashamed of me.

Suddenly, we heard horses' hooves. Our peasant driver slowed down. There was nothing to do but wait and pray that whoever was astride the horse was friendly. They turned out to be a couple of Polish sentries. Father tried to explain our situation. He spoke Polish but they couldn't understand his pronunciation. In the few words of Polish that I knew, I tried to tell them that I was an American and Father was taking me back to my country. The whole thing must have sounded very peculiar: I am sure they had never met a little girl who was an American, spoke Russian, with a father who had a strange, toneless speech on a hay wagon. But they looked reasonable, and whether it was my pleading or my father's condition or our prayers, they decided to escort us across to the border town where we would be kept in jail until a decision was made as to what to do with us.

The jail was small, with a couple of drunks inside. The jail keeper let us sit by the stove and gave us some bread and hot milk. Another official who spoke Russian interviewed Father and me and we told him about Mother and the other children and that we expected them to cross the border and join us. He sent a man to get them.

For two days we waited in jail—the most wonderful two days I had ever had with my father. He sat with his arm around me, and between whispering and writing, taught me how to cope with life. He said that everything we got out of it—joy, love, pleasure, happiness—depended completely on our individual awareness and attitude. He said the proper attitude was the most important thing he could give me. When I questioned him about all the horrors, injustice and cruelty—about his wound— and told him how much I hated those who had inflicted pain on us, he told me not to waste a single moment hating anything.

"Always look forward, never back," he said. "Don't waste your life while you're planning it. Don't make a wastebasket of your brain. Unclutter it, take out the trash." He told me that my life was ahead of me. I was their talisman, and he believed that we would get to America.

It was a happy reunion when my mother burst into the jail with the children. She showed them my American midwife's certificate, and, although there was nothing they could do—we were illegally in Poland—they were willing to let us proceed to the next town, Rovno, which was larger.

There my father had to be held in jail until Mother could prove our intentions and rights. Mother, Rosalie, Nucy and I wound up in a filthy rented room with one bed. I slept on the floor with Rosalie on a hay mattress and Mother in the one bed with Nucy. Our clothes were getting shabbier, and the lice and bedbugs had crawled into the seams of our clothes. Between the bedbugs and the lice, I had constant resort to kerosene, pouring it over Rosalie's head and mine, while Mother cooked our food, took care of the baby, and made pilgrimages to officials to beg for our release.

Father remained in jail. We were terribly afraid that he would die there; we couldn't visit him. The guards permitted him to come to the window and wave to us. Every day I carried a pail of food to him because Mother and I were in horrible fear that the jail food would make him ill. We knew at least that he was alive.

It was my chore to scrub the floor of our room. I had to go to the well with two large pails, fill them, and carry them back. I learned to carry the bar that held the two pails across my shoulders. It usually took me about three trips. The water had to be used for cooking as well as washing. We battled the lice and bedbugs constantly, and our clothes were taking a beating. Just to keep clean was a horrendous job. Somehow we got through the winter and summer. Our greatest luxury was a cake of soap. It looked like very hard, white and blue marble. It was hard, rough and foul-smelling, but to this day I can't bear to throw away a scrap of soap. I cannot walk out of a plane without taking a sliver with me. I might be paying $100 a day for a hotel room, but the soap goes with me.

In Rovno, Mother learned that the American Embassy was in

Warsaw. The American Ambassador to Poland was Hugh Gibson, and she wrote to him, telling him of our plight. Months later, we received a note from the Embassy, telling us to hold on, not to lose heart. The information, they said, had been forwarded to the Board of Health in New York, where every birth was registered, and as soon as they could find the record of my birth, they would see how I could be issued a passport. Christmas 1920 came and went. We had been in Poland a year.

I don't know how we stood it in our skimpy clothes. The children were growing out of theirs and Mother was afraid to spend our precious small capital. But every once in a while she was forced to. I would be left with the kids while she went on a mysterious trip and came back minus another piece of jewelry.

The jail guards allowed us to exchange notes with Father. Then, after three months, they allowed us to visit him once a week. Finally, in February 1921, they released him. He was worn and thin and had aged terribly. My heart ached every time I saw him, but his eyes were always bright and he gave us courage.

Soon after his release we got a letter from the American Embassy. My birth certificate verification had arrived. Hope sprang in our hearts again, as we started for Warsaw.

The 4th of July came again. For years I hadn't had a birthday celebration or gone to a party. Mother again reminded me what July 4th meant to us and what it meant to America. I was losing heart and courage. It seemed so unlikely that I would see the longed-for day when my feet would touch down on American soil, but I lived with expectation and an ache in the pit of my stomach, waiting and watching for the mail in Warsaw.

My shoes were worn, and my feet had outgrown them. Since I had to do most of the walking, Mother decided I would have to have a new pair of shoes. We would just have to spare the money. Most of Mother's jewelry was still intact; she had sold only three pieces. She gave me a few pieces of Polish money and told me that I was a big girl and would have to buy the shoes myself.

I scrubbed my face and went off on my first shopping venture. It was very serious and I felt quite important. I was a real grownup, shopping for a very special occasion. I must have looked in a dozen stores before I made my final decision. I fell in love with a pair of white canvas, high heeled shoes. I think the salesman doubted my choice, but I was a customer, so he let me have them. I squeezed my feet into them, paid for them and walked out of the store, leaving my tattered shoes behind.

I had never been in high heels before. After about three blocks, I couldn't stand or balance myself. The cobblestones of the streets of Warsaw were no place to walk with high heels. I took the shoes off, sat on the curb, and wondered how I would get my hot, swollen feet back into them. I wanted to cry, I was in such pain. Finally, I crammed my feet back into the shoes and tried to stumble home, but I couldn't stand the agony. I took them off and walked home barefoot. My feet were blistered and I was miserable. I knew I had made a mistake and was afraid to face Mother.

But, bless her, instead of scolding me she thought it hysterically funny. There were so few laughs in our lives in those days that when she started to laugh at the sight of me, I started to laugh too. Rosalie, who didn't know what we were laughing about, started to laugh with us. It was a wonderful release. Finally, Mother said, "Now that you've bought them, you'll have to learn to live with them. This will teach you not to be in such a hurry." She was in wonderful humor, filled with excitement, because she had been waiting with great news. The precious letter had finally come. I would be given my U.S. passport.

Father came in carrying Nucy. He looked at me—my skirt didn't fit; it was above my knees. He said, "Our princess has grown up." I had grown three inches since we left Russia. It seems strange that during all the privations, physical hard work, cooking and cleaning, I still had grown three inches in a little over a year and a half. I had been barely four feet five inches when I left Russia and was now four feet eight inches. Now I felt grown up with my new shoes.

Clutching our meager possesions, we left and went straight to the Embassy. Father didn't have to go back to jail. We were under American protective custody—I was an American citizen. It was just a question of getting my passport. The day I got it we had my picture taken. It was May 27, 1921; Nucy was two, Rosalie was almost eight, and I was almost fourteen. Mother kept going to the Polish authorities with my passport, trying to plead with them to issue the rest of the family Polish passports, to allow them to get out of Poland. It was a miracle but she succeeded. By July 27, two months after I got mine, she persuaded the Poles that Father was actually Polish because in January 1880 the borderline had been Polish territory. My parents' passports were finally issued. When we looked at the spelling of the names, we were astonished to realize that each country translates foreign names as it sees fit. Mine and my parents didn't match, but what difference did it make, said Mother, as long as they let us go. From the Russian spelling Barandyc, my parents became Brandos, and I became Barondess (copied from my birth certificate).

I am told that Warsaw is a beautiful city. I don't remember anything about it except the American Embassy, and that was the most beautiful building in the world to me. Red Cross headquarters provided us with a room, and I loved every minute of it because it was a step nearer our goal. The room was modest but clean. Father gained a little weight and the desperation went out of Mother's eyes. We had to wait, but no one was going to send us back.

Although the letter from the Embassy and my passport released us as far as the Polish government was concerned, there was still much red tape. The U.S. Embassy had to find our relatives in the United States.

The Embassy staff took one look at the tattered rags we were wearing and sent us to the American Red Cross, where they gave us all sweaters. Mother splurged and bought me my first dress since Russia. My Red Cross pullover must have been knitted by loving hands for a soldier at least six feet two, because it came down to my knees. The olive drab khaki color was not what one would choose for a fourteen-year-old girl, but I thought it the most beautiful present I ever got. It was my first import—made in the U.S.A., knitted by loving hands during the war.

Our next stop was Berlin, where my parents told me I fell out of my carriage when I was six months old, at the top of the stairs of the Berlin railroad station. They talked with animation about the way my father caught me and saved my life. Now I was saving theirs by just being alive. Berlin was only a railroad stop, and then Antwerp. Belgium was the first place we saw where people looked normal and clean. No one loooked frightened, beaten, or hungry. I ate my first banana and saw a tangerine again. There seemed to be excitement everywhere and my heart was light.

Our next stop was England, the last stop separating us from our goal. I counted the minutes to make the hours go faster. I wanted to hear English spoken by everyone so I could feel the sound of the language that was going to be mine. When we got to England we took a train to Liverpool, arriving late on a foggy and drizzly evening. The air was penetratingly cold. The English I heard sounded strange. I realized that I didn't understand a word. Liverpool looked ugly; the chimney pots were silhouetted against the dark foggy sky and there was an ominous, unfriendly feeling. I guess the feeling reached us all. The family was silent until we arrived at our lodgings. It was a boarding house in the middle of town.

The proprietor was a jovial, red-faced man who received us with a welcome smile. The place was clean and bright and smelled fresh. Somehow there was an atmosphere of home. The moment the door closed behind us, our gloom vanished. We were shown to a nice, large room with two beds and a small room next to it, with a tub in the bathroom right outside and a piece of white soap—I couldn't believe it. I could take a bath; we could all take a bath! I asked my mother if I could please be last, so I could lie down in the white tub filled with the warm water.

This time I didn't have to carry the pails of water. I could have plenty of it, up to my neck and use the white soap.

I went into the little room that Rosalie and I were to share. The brass bed looked divine and the linen sheets so clean! It was one year and nine months since we had climbed through the window of my room. For the first time I was going to have a bath in a private bathroom and sleep in a real, proper bed all by myself.

Mother was giving the girls a bath. There was glee and laughter and the splashing of water. In the other room I saw my father stretched out on the bed, staring at the ceiling. By the expression on his face, he seemed to be praying. I tiptoed back and lay down on my bed to wait for my turn. Mother finished bathing the children, then Father took his bath. Then she took hers, and finally the bathroom was all mine.

I couldn't wait for the tub to fill, so I stepped into about five inches of water. The sensation was tremendous. In this case, realization topped anticipation. As the water rose, it felt as if it were a pile of heavenly feathers, and I stretched in sensuous pleasure. I suddenly looked at myself and was startled. There had been no privacy, no mirrors, and no opportunity or time to really see myself since we had left Russia. What I saw was not the scrawny little girl with two little buds, but a young woman with tiny breasts.

The shock was great. I didn't know whether I liked it. I felt awkward. There I was, in-between again. My childhood was gone; I didn't belong with the children or the grownups, and I missed my contemporaries, who were God knew where. Would I ever see them again? I suddenly thought of all of them and wondered what they looked like now. My throat tightened with a lump. I thought of my father's favorite prayer and realized that there was no time for tears, no time to be sorry. Instead, I washed my hair and gave myself the pleasure of a second soaping.

Lying down naked on the clean, cool, linen sheets and tired

of all the thinking and planning, I closed my eyes and drifted into luxurious sleep, letting go as if I were suspended in air.

The next morning was my first English lesson: "Please," "Thank you," and "Bread and butter." Then my parents went off to check our passage while I stayed with the children. Father and Mother came back very happy. Everything was set; the ship was sailing the next day. The boarding time was early morning. The two children were too small to understand what was happening, but they caught the spirit, looked happy, and went to sleep.

It was still dark when my mother got us all together for a fast washing and some breakfast. She checked and rechecked our meager belongings. I put my panties on and felt for my emerald earrings in the belt. It was my second pair of panties since leaving Russia. The first pair I had outgrown, and the emeralds were resewn into the new ones. The nice proprietor helped us out and wished us good luck, a good journey, as we left on the way to the boat.

I had never seen a large ship or been in a seaport before. It was exciting and fascinating to watch the bustle and confusion of embarkation. We got in line to board, Father and Mother first. Father had Nucy by the hand. They arranged that he would handle the passports but she would do the talking, so that no one would hear his peculiar, whispering speech. Rosalie and I were behind them as we finally walked up the gangplank. A uniformed officer at the top of the stairs was checking the people as they boarded. We were perhaps only five feet from him, and Father was holding the passports in one hand, when suddenly Nucy broke away, running toward Rosalie and me. Mother turned to tell me to grab her hand. My father was standing in front of the officer, who asked his name. Father hesitated; the officer repeated his question. Mother breathlessly cut in to answer the officer, and I saw the look of desperate helplessness in Father's face, as the officer said to Mother, "What is the matter with your husband? Can't he speak?"

I caught my breath and looked at Mother's face. She exchanged a look with Father and the agony was very plain. I couldn't understand what was being said—the man was speaking English—but I understood the gesture when he asked us to step aside. While another officer was summoned to examine us, we waited for the twenty longest minutes I ever experienced in my life, while people went through showing their passports, giving their names, and having no trouble at all. My mother begged and pleaded. She explained what was wrong with Father—that he had been wounded but was all right—with no success. I watched our possessions as they were returned to the dock. We sat huddled together in silence as the gangplank was pulled away and the ship sailed without us.

The next couple of weeks were a nightmare. We were trapped all over again. There was no turning back. We were advised to go to London. What now?

We got a room in London. I watched the kids while Mother and Father went to the American Embassy again to repeat our story. Sometimes all of us went, so Mother could show me to them as living proof of the piece of paper that said I was born in the United States. We were a peculiar problem; Father was examined by doctors again and again.

Finally, we got the divine dispensation. We boarded another ship, the *Celtic*, steerage class, from Dover, on August 27, 1921. We stood on the deck waiting for the precious moment when the gangplank would be taken away. This time we weren't gay; we were grim until we heard the cry, "All aboard going aboard—All ashore going ashore."

The boat started moving and we were really on our way. I clutched the rail. As I turned to look at my father and mother, they were holding hands. Tears were streaming down their faces, and Mother was whispering, "In God's good and blessed hour, in God's good and blessed hour, in God's good and blessed hour."

CHAPTER FOUR

All Aboard—Ellis Island

THE *Celtic* was a small ship of the White Star Line. We had had second-class passage on the first ship. On this one we were in steerage. It rained and stormed for most of the time we were at sea, a very rough crossing. Mother and the children were seasick and couldn't eat, but Father and I were miraculously fine. In the rough muggy weather, our cabin, down in the belly of the ship, was cramped, humid and hot. It didn't matter, though. The vibration and noise of the ship made the most beautiful symphony I have ever heard. Nothing could stifle the sheer joy of the thought that we had left Russia and privations behind us.

After a couple of days, the captain, having heard our story, sent an officer down to invite us to come up to visit second class and have the privileges of the dining room. We were, of course, very happy with that, but Mother was too sick to eat; it made no difference to her. Father and I had a few meals there. Everybody was kind to us, and we were taken on a tour of the first class sections. There I saw again lovely women dressed in evening clothes and heard lively music. The people looked so clean. This seemed like a fantasy. I wondered if I would ever travel first class on a boat, wear evening clothes, dance, and eat beautiful food. But it wasn't a dream—all those things would happen. My father said they would because I was going where I belonged.

The last night on board, my father allowed me to stay on deck fairly late. I watched the moon play on the great ocean and listened to the turn of the engines as the ship cut through the water. I looked so hard—we wanted to see the very first glimpse of the promised land. Excitement mounted inside me, but finally I knew I had to go below and try to get some sleep.

I sneaked into my bunk next to Rosalie and lay there in the dark. Everyone was sound asleep. I listened to the steady sound of the engines. I wished it were morning—waiting was agony. Counting to sixty for each minute to make the time go faster, my heart beat quickly, *thum, thum, thum,* almost in unison with the steady revolution of the engines. I wanted to get up on deck again and feel the caress of the wind on my face and body.

I was afraid to move for fear of awakening everyone, so I tried to think of other things to make the time pass. I tried to imagine the wonders of New York, a special kind of fairyland, with tall buildings like colored candy sticks, with beams of sunrays washing them with gold, and always in front of it the Statue of Liberty, silhouetted against the skyline and looking large, solid and safe, saying in her regal isolation, "I am here; everything is well; everything will be all right now."

Rosalie's little body next to me was very hot. The sheets were damp, clammy and rough. The bunk was too narrow for me to move away from her, so I tried to recall my own room in Russia—the cool, clean feel of linen sheets in my own soft bed in my room where I had the luxury of privacy. It seemed so long ago. I closed my eyes as I used to when they had to be pasted together, and suddenly I could see every inch of that large room, with a door at each end. My bed, a chest, a mirror, a wardrobe, a small table-desk with Lena's beautiful silver icon, and a comfortable chair. The room had one large window with a low bookcase under the sill, filled with my books and dolls. But the most important was the electric light with the pushbutton, over my painted bed.

I remembered how my father used to call me the "Princess," because I was so fussy about my bed. Finally I had what I wanted—all those pillows and all those perinas. The window faced the edge of the orchard, and about six feet away was *my* tree, the largest and oldest black cherry tree. I knew every branch of it. Every morning it was the first thing I feasted my eyes on. In spring, it awoke with dark green foliage and white blossoms, and then came the beautiful red fruit with the greatest perfume I've ever known.

My cousin Volodya and a couple of my chums would be allowed to pick and sort the cherries for preserving. Each of us would be given an apron with a large pocket in front. We climbed the tree and competed to see how fast we could pick. While picking, we ate all that our stomachs could stand. The farmhands picked the rest of the orchard, but this tree was mine; no one else touched it. Each of us would fall out of the tree at least once. But, miraculously, no one was ever hurt beyond a few scratches and an occasional sprain. We got hot and sticky, and we laughed and screamed, usually ending up with no dinner, but it was worth it. In the house, the cook had a large copper pot ready for us. Our next job was to sort the cherries, putting the largest and best aside. We pitted the large ones with a straight pin. It was a feat to get the pit out without bruising or breaking the cherry. Then, a piece of walnut was placed inside, and those were preserved in sugar to make the most delicious delicacies for special occasions. The rest were used for cherry jam and cherry brandy.

I remembered the day that Volodya and I fell from the cherry tree. Lying in the bunk, I wondered what had happened to him and the rest of the family. I felt sad, because I knew I would never see them again. Suddenly Rosalie moved, and the smell of cherries vanished. My hands were no longer sticky and hot and my first love and my room were gone. I was lying in the dark in the smelly steerage bunk in the belly of the ship—no longer a little girl picking cherries or secretly reading books until dawn. Everything seemed suspended—I still didn't belong anywhere, didn't belong in the past and was a little frightened of the future. The memories of luxury and comfort and laughter and childhood were so far away that they didn't seem real.

I was over fourteen years old. I had lost four years somewhere. My childhood was gone forever. I longed to speak to my father about my feelings, but that was too difficult. And I was at that awkward, terrible, painful time of a girl's life when she can't talk to her mother. Too old for toys and too young for boys.

I felt trapped that night. I felt deaf and dumb and prayed for sleep, but none came. If only I could go out on deck and look at the stars. . . . It would be so comfortable to find the Big Dipper; it was always where it was supposed to be. Wherever I was, I could pretend I was lying in a hammock and all this was a bad dream. If only I could take my icon out and look at it. I wanted to cry but couldn't.

Suddenly fear clutched my heart. Suppose they wouldn't let us stay in America. What would happen to us? Where could we go? "No, no, no," I said to myself and prayed, "God grant me the serenity to accept the things I cannot change, the courage to change the things I can, and the wisdom to know the difference." But my mind was saying, "Don't think about anything."

Squeezing my eyes shut, I tried to see the kaleidoscope in the ice-cream parlor's great silver balls, but no relief came. I repeated the prayer until out of sheer exhaustion I must have finally fallen asleep. Suddenly my mother was shaking me saying, "Marishka, get up, we're here!"

We dressed silently and quickly. We were the first up on deck for the inspection of passports. We hoped that some of my mother's family would be there to meet us. The Red Cross in Warsaw had inserted an ad for my parents in the New York papers to find Mother's brothers and sisters. Her family had no other way of knowing that we had escaped from Russia and were arriving, but the Red Cross found them. They were going to meet us. This was the end of the struggle—our last stop.

I peeked at the Statue of Liberty, my first friend, as we waited in line to have our passports checked. The land was so near and yet seemed so far. When would this endless waiting end? When would we be able to just sit and know that we were home? And soon, after all we had gone through.

Because we had traveled in steerage, we had to go through quarantine, and as soon as we were off the *Celtic* and on the Manhattan dock, we were taken in a ferry boat to Ellis Island. We were told that our relatives would see us there.

We stepped off the boat and in the midday sunlight saw before us an enormous building of red and white stone, with arches and turrets. Surely this was the fairy castle of my dreams, our welcome to the promised land. But a few moments later we were brought inside, and we found no enchanted corridors but enormous dark official rooms, a dungeon filled with murmuring and shuffling people, our fellow passengers questioned and inspected by the immigration men.

We had to climb long flights of stairs to an enormous room where light streamed from high, dirty windows.

There was a sound of muffled sobs as people formed lines to be tagged like animals with a number. They were speaking so many languages that it sounded like Babel. The air was humid and stale, and muffled cries of fear permeated the room. This was the cruelest reception my shattered young heart could ever have imagined.

The helpless immigrants were herded into groups. Official clerks asked hundreds of questions to determine background, moral character, and health. This small island in New York Harbor seemed only a few yards away from the small island where the Statue of Liberty stood with her torch of freedom.

The authorities said that Father would have to go through a physical examination in the men's section, and that we would have to go to the women's section.

It wasn't the first time that I saw my father look dejected, but this time he also looked beaten and discouraged. "Not again," said my mother, as she threw her arms around his neck and cried, "Not here. Not again. We will be sent back." The more desperately she moaned, the less frightened my father became. He stood there for a moment, pulled himself up to his five feet ten, and said, in his strange whisper, "Mother, God got us out of Russia and he will get us out of here. We're home. Nobody will send us back. They can't. We have suffered enough. Please hang on, darling, hang on. We'll make it."

Mother looked at me, dried her tears, put her arms around the two small children, and took us to be examined. Father had to stay under observation, for they didn't believe him when he tried to explain that his defective voice was due to a bullet wound. The silver tube in his windpipe, after the tracheotomy—now in common use for cancer of the throat—was not a familiar sight in those days. Our situation was complicated; I was an American citizen who could not be deported. I was under age. My father seemed to be an invalid, and they were afraid he would be a ward of the state. They couldn't deport me, and they couldn't separate me from my family unless a friend or relative, with my parents' consent, would take charge of me. My parents' application for citizenship, applied for before I was born, had expired because they had stayed out of the country more than seven years.

In the meantime, my mother's family—brothers and sisters—found us. When they saw where we were to sleep, on double bunks made out of wirelike cages, with one hard pillow and two khaki blankets on each, they were appalled.

After several examinations of my father's heart and his general physical condition, doctors found that he was strong and healthy except for his throat and speech. But they kept us there, trying to work this problem out. We spent fourteen days at Ellis Island, eating in the mess hall. As I gazed at the Statue of Liberty from the island, or at lower Manhattan to the east, New York was so near that I could almost touch it—and yet it seemed a million miles away.

My uncles were gentle and tried to comfort us, but we were numb. How I wanted to get off that island and see America! The temptation was great. I could have walked off—my uncles and aunts were willing to take me—but I was determined that I wouldn't leave my parents for one minute. The immigration authorities would have deported my parents, I thought, had I gone off. I stuck like plaster. The authorities were stymied. Father, with his disability, certainly didn't look as if he could support a wife and three children. We pleaded that we had a little money, but they didn't think it was enough.

One day, after we had been there a couple of days, Uncle Bob, my mother's brother, arrived with a plan. There was a man living in New York, very highly thought of, very prominent, whose name happened to be almost the same as ours. He was Joseph Barondess, an educator and a liberal philanthropist. Since the name of Barondess was not common, my uncle thought that if they appealed to him and asked him to intervene for us, he might be able to help. Perhaps he was related to us? My father did know of a distant relationship and he was willing to grasp at any straw, so he told my uncles the particulars. Uncle Bob went to see Joseph Barondess to tell him our story, and Uncle Irving went to a Louis Brandeis, whose name was the German version of ours. (We had relatives in Germany who used that spelling.) Joseph Barondess had a son whose name was the same as my father's, Benjamin. Maybe because of that, or because he was a great human being interested in other people, he decided to use his influence to help us. He appealed to President Harding for his intervention. With miraculous speed, within a few days we were released. The immigration law at that time was that any child born on American soil who was under age could have one parent appointed as guardian. My father became mine. Mother and the children were able to come with him.

Finally we got word—we were free. Of course, not without one more little drama. By then, we were getting used to any situation. We never believed that we would walk through any door until after we were through it. Two days before our departure, Rosalie developed a high fever. On the day of our release she broke out in red spots. The doctor said she had the measles. Naturally, the doctor couldn't let her go with us. She had to be quarantined. After a quick conference it was agreed that the little eight-year-old girl was to be taken to a city hospital.

A lovely, large black nurse came to take her away. Rosalie's little eyes looked desperate and frightened; her poor face was swollen and red. She was in tears and delirious, but we knew it was only for a few days. So, with her torn from us, in a strange place, and a strange country, we walked off Ellis Island, the four of us, my mother muttering again, "In the good and blessed hour, in the good and blessed hour," as I stepped onto the "soil" of New York City.

CHAPTER FIVE

Brooklyn, U.S.A.

WE WERE whisked into a car, the four of us squeezed in with my uncles and the pathetic luggage. I couldn't see a thing. Rain was pouring and I vaguely remember going over a bridge. By the time we reached the area in Brooklyn where my grandmother lived, the rain had subsided. We were on a street of shabby stoop-front houses. Grandmother lived on the ground floor of one of them. We were ushered into the kitchen, which had wooden chairs and a table covered with oil cloth. Grandmother's excitement at seeing my mother, the chattering and crying and kissing, mixed with hugging and tears, sounded like the Tower of Babel.

We were offered cheese, sausages, bread, cookies, tea and milk. The whole family crowded into the kitchen. My mother's two sisters were there, Tilly and Pauline. I was dying to see the other rooms, and when I realized that I'd been forgotten, after a few minutes I started exploring by myself. The next room was the living room; next to it was a small bedroom with one bed. That was obviously my grandmother's bedroom. The living room furniture had been rearranged and crowded to hold two extra beds, one for my father and mother and another for Nucy and Rosalie. It was obvious that I was to sleep on the overstuffed sofa. Rosalie was still in the hospital.

When I came back to the kitchen, they were still talking, laughing, crying. Nucy fell asleep from sheer exhaustion. I sat in the corner, unable to understand a word of what was being said—a potpourri of English, Russian, and Yiddish. I had never heard Yiddish before, and the few words of Russian were not enough to include me in the conversation. I realized that they still thought of me as a child. I was fourteen years old and I hadn't been a child for a long time.

That night I lay on the hard, overstuffed sofa covered with my blanket and stifled my sobs so my parents wouldn't hear me. I felt alone, rejected and betrayed. Ever since I could remember, my parents had told me of the beauties of America. All I could think of now, in this crowded, dreary place, was our home in Russia. It seemed like a magic palace by comparison: the beautiful French furniture in the living room; the dining room with its long sideboard and table long enough to seat twelve; the gleaming silver samovar and the sparkling glassware; the view of the gorgeous orchards and private lake; my own room; our cook, Olga, and Lena; the ritual of bread baking and jam making; my school friends and elegant family; the lovely summer dacha, sleigh riding in the winter on the blinding white snow. My heart was heavy. My ride to Brooklyn certainly hadn't revealed any forests or country. As I twisted on that uncomfortable sofa sobbing my heart out, I wondered if from now on I would have nothing but memories. My thoughts went back to swimming in the river, the picnics on the beach when we caught the crayfish and boiled them, watching them turn from brown-black to a wonderful lobster red. Through my salty tears, I remembered the taste of the sweet meat. The years of horror that we spent were completely forgotten; all I remembered was the beauty of Russia.

I must have cried most of the night. When I finally did fall asleep my throat was sore. In the morning my mother tried to wake me. But I couldn't open my eyes; they were glued shut.

She called Father. At first they thought I had caught Rosalie's measles, but, after a few minutes of confusion and conference, they figured out I must have cried myself to sleep. They put cold wet towels on my face, and after a half hour or so the swelling subsided and my eyes opened. I looked as if I had been stung by a hive of bees. This had been my first day in the blessed land I was born in. It was November 1921.

After a few days of moping, Mother said that we were going to visit my Aunt Pauline and her husband, Dr. Lessinger. I never learned his first name. When he got his medical degree, he became "My husband the doctor," or "My father the doctor." The train ride to the Bronx took two hours. It was noisy and crowded; Mother managed to get a seat and held Nucy in her lap. The weather was still overcast and drizzly. I was chilled and still depressed. I stood near the back platform with my father, trying to look out the window, searching for the promised beauty and drama of New York. But on this gloomy day, all I saw were chimney stacks, billboards, and tenements. The stacks looked bleak; I couldn't read the billboards. America the Beautiful? I had been betrayed.

I looked at my father, and he took my hand without a word. I think he could read my thoughts. The people on the train didn't look worried and frightened like the ones I saw in Russia and Poland, but they were seriously occupied, rushing on and off the train. Some were reading the papers but they never looked at each other. They never smiled and didn't seem very friendly or attractive. As far as I was concerned, this was an endless ride to nowhere.

I missed Rosalie. She was still in the hospital and we weren't to see her for a few more days. My mother stared into space silently. The reaction to the long, miserable years seemed to be setting into her expression, too. Even her spirits were dampening.

The Bronx didn't look any better to me than Brooklyn. The doctor's home was a little better than Grandmother's but I thought it ugly. Pauline and the doctor had two young daughters, Esther and Jean, who silently sat and stared at us through the whole visit. I couldn't understand English, so there was nothing to do but sit and listen to my parents talk to my aunt and uncle. Finally, we were fed and they gave us some clothes. By now any hand-me-down was welcome. I was still wearing my shabby, now too short and too tight dress that mother had bought me in Poland. It was incredible, but I was growing like a weed. The Red Cross khaki sweater that had been down to my knees when I got it was four inches shorter.

My aunt gave me a navy blue pleated serge skirt and a midi blouse with a white sailor collar. I looked like a tub in the pleated skirt, although I had been used to wearing almost the same thing when I went to school. It was like our Marinskya Gymnasia uniform. But then my figure had been a child's figure, and now the sailor collar just didn't look right and I hated it, although at this point I should have gladly welcomed a potato sack. After looking myself over, I came to the conclusion that the midi blouse might be a blessing; it covered my growing bosom that I just couldn't get used to, and I tried everything I knew to minimize it.

The ride home seemed endless. After the two years we spent glued together every minute of the day and night, living in one room except for the separation from my father when he was in jail, I suddenly felt like a deaf mute, lost and bewildered. I couldn't feel part of anything. My parents were busy with strange relatives who talked in a language I didn't understand. It was obvious from the look of horror on the faces of the people listening that my mother was repeating our story over and over. I could tell by the look they gave my father that they wondered how he could take care of his family. Everything seemed unreal. I hoped that Aladdin would come with his magic lamp and transport me on a magic carpet back to Russia. Russia by this time seemed so much better than this. I was convinced that we were the poor relatives whom no one really wanted.

Rosalie finally came out of the hospital. Her little face was round and pale and the look in her eyes told of the anguish she had been through. She was so happy to see us. With tears of joy she told us she felt abandoned and didn't believe that she would ever see us again. It was a happy reunion.

There was nothing for me to read or do. There weren't any Russian books around, and I couldn't read the ones in English. My parents sold most of my mother's jewelry and managed to get some money together. Everyone was looking for some kind of business that my father could get into. Some of the relatives agreed to lend him some money. Mother was not equipped to work; she had never done anything in her life but trim hats. I was too young. Obviously no one would give Father an ordinary job. After two weeks we heard of a small candy store that sold stationery and newspapers on Ditmas Avenue in Brooklyn. It had living quarters in back. Since I had to be enrolled in school, and there was no time to lose, Father made a fast decision to buy the store. After we were in it for a week he saw that the inventory had been padded, that it wasn't worth half of what he paid for it. He had been cheated, but, in his usual way, he determined to make the best of it.

When we moved into the two filthy rooms in the back, scrubbing this mess was left to me. I learned about scouring powder and Lysol, and it kept me busy for days. Knowing my fastidious father, I worked without a whimper. The relatives managed to get us a couple of chairs, a table, two beds, and a narrow folding cot. In addition to a small, terrible bathroom, we had a tiny room just big enough to take one double bed for my parents. The one other room, which served as a bedroom for Nucy and Rosalie in one bed and the folding cot for me, was also our kitchen and living room.

I was enrolled in public school, a typical, nice red brick building two blocks away from the store. Father wrote the principal a letter which he handed her when he took me there. The principal explained that if I started in kindergarten and was as bright as described in the letter, I would learn the ABC's with the kindergarten faster, and as soon as I learned them I would be promoted or skipped until I caught up with children of my own age.

The first classroom I walked into was filled with five- and six-year-olds. After we watched teacher write "dog" and "cat" on the blackboard, the kids looked at me and whispered among themselves. I heard another phrase I didn't understand, "Big dope." When school broke for lunch, children in other classrooms found out from the little ones that I was in kindergarten. They tried to talk to me, but I couldn't answer, so they tagged me with another epithet, "Greenhorn." The look of contempt and ridicule on their little faces made me feel worse.

I wanted to run away, but I didn't know where to go. I wanted to kill myself, but I didn't know how. I wished there was some place I could go to, like the wheat fields, and think it out, but there was no place to go. I was afraid to walk down the street alone; I knew I'd be lost without English, and my insides felt like a wrung-out mop.

When school was over, I walked home. As I neared the store I saw my father standing in front of the newspaper stand, smiling at the people as they stopped to buy the papers, but his eyes looked sad and beaten. Mother was behind the counter, selling candy to some children. I couldn't believe it. Was this the culmination of the stories and dreams of the glorious, comfortable world that would erase the horrible years? How could my parents have made such a mistake? Yet in my heart I knew that they felt just as trapped as I was, and my heart ached for them.

I walked into the dismal back room and saw the dirty pots and pans that my mother had left on the stove. She wasn't used to housekeeping. The years she had spent in Russia pampered with servants hadn't helped make her a good housekeeper. She was terribly disorganized in the kitchen, and now that she had to help in the store, she was worse. I took the pots out to the little backyard where I sat down among the dead weeds and leaves and started to scrub. My mother came out and stood looking at me.

"You told me America was beautiful," I said. "We had such a beautiful home in Russia. Why did you want to come back here? Maybe the Bolsheviks would have been all right."

Mother didn't say a word, but gave me a pathetic, helpless look. I wanted to cry but I couldn't; I had cried myself out.

On a Sunday morning one of my aunts came to keep my mother company, and Father said that we were going on a little excursion, just he and I. He said, "I will show you beautiful New York."

I didn't believe there was any such thing as beautiful New York. A couple of blocks away was the elevated station where we had taken the train to the Bronx. It happened to be a lovely day, sunny and crisp. There was a slight breeze. I wore my midi blouse and skirt and a winter jacket that my parents had brought me. My father took me by the hand and we went to the train which wasn't crowded. In about an hour we got off at Fifth Avenue and Sixtieth Street.

When we walked up the stairs out of the subway the sun hit my eyes, and then I saw the Plaza Hotel, the brilliant square, and the green grass and trees of Central Park. Carriages and horses waited to take people for rides through the park. It was breathtaking. We walked down Fifth Avenue, the wide street lined with stunning shops. My face lit up with wonder. Father looked at me and said, "You see, darling, I didn't fool you. This is a beautiful city; we just live in the wrong part of it, only a hour away. We can't afford to live here now, but you will some day. The wonderful part about your country is that it's all up to you. Your whole lifetime is in front of you if you will listen, learn to apply yourself, remember to use the first commandment, the Golden Rule, the prayers I taught you. You can become anything you want to in the United States—except the President, because you're a girl." We both laughed . . . our first joyous laughter in America.

"You won't be in the low grades long. My princess is smart." He took me to an Automat and showed me the mechanical wonder I'd heard about in my childhood. He wanted to take me to one more place, where unfortunately we couldn't spend much time, because he couldn't leave Mother alone too long. He wanted me to see it so I would be able to find my way there later. We turned back up Fifth Avenue and walked many blocks to the Metropolitan Museum. A fast hour through its halls was too much. My head swam. We came back to Fifth Avenue and before taking the subway back to Brooklyn we sat down on a bench at the entrance to the park zoo at 63rd Street. I looked eastward along 63rd Street and saw a row of beautiful townhouses. This was the "Silk-stocking District." The brownstones, with polished brass rails, were neat and handsome.

I said, "Do you think we could ever live here?" Father's answer was, "I can't promise that we could live here together, but if you remember what I taught you, you may live here someday. It's all right to expect the best of everything, but make the best of everything you get; don't ever be unhappy and waste your life while you're planning."

I took a good look at 63rd Street; I wanted to etch it in my mind. Then I closed my eyes and made a wish. I threw an imaginary boomerang. I thought, when I grow up, please God, send this boomerang back to me so I can be on 63rd Street. Suddenly I was full of hope again and life was beautiful.

The ride back to Brooklyn seemed like nothing at all. I was going back with determination and purpose. I was going to show these school kids that I wasn't a big dope. My father said I could do it, and I would have a race with them. He said we needed a plan and teamwork. We agreed that we'd never speak a word of Russian at home again, only English. He said, "It won't be easy, but nothing easy is worth while."

My parents worked hard. We stuck to our plan. Three months later we moved from the back of the store to a flat a few doors down, on the second floor of the corner building. This apartment had four rooms and a kitchen. Nucy, Rosalie, and I had a bedroom. There was a living room and a small dining room. Our parents had the other bedroom, and there was a good big bathroom. It was heaven.

The store had tripled its business. People went out of their way to buy from my father. It fast became known that this superior man who had been wounded in Russia was selling newspapers, and my father was encouraged. Two days after our excursion to the Metropolitan Museum and Fifth Avenue, I was moved out of kindergarten. Then I went from class to class until I was in the seventh grade in a little over three months. To get to the eighth grade was a little tougher—it took the next three months.

I graduated from public school in June 1922, seven months from the day I entered it, and faced my first summer vacation in America. At fifteen I was growing like a weed and began appreciating the importance of money. Watching my father and mother putting the pennies and nickels and dimes together to buy our bare necessities gave me a sense of values.

I mentioned to a friend that I wanted a summer job and was introduced to a neighbor who manufactured men's neckties. He asked me how old I was. I said proudly, "I'll be fifteen next month." He looked me over and suggested that I could take a box of neckties on consignment to lower Broadway in Manhattan where there were a lot of men's stores. I was to look in the windows, he said, and if they showed no neckties I was to go inside and ask the salesmen if they would buy some. He added, "A pretty girl like you will have no problem, and you could earn some money without having to get a work permit. You can keep 50 percent of the amount you sell."

So I had my first job in the Land of Opportunity.

Nucy, by natural Americanization, was renamed Lucy. It sounded just like Nucy. Rosalie was in school. They were both instant Americans.

CHAPTER SIX

Outside Looking In

I TOOK the subway to Broadway—I knew how by then. With the large box of ties under my arm, I walked into a store. The salesman looked surprised to see a girl. After I explained in my accented English that I was on school vacation, only six months in America, he called all the men who worked there, including the proprietor, and I sold twenty ties. My selling spiel was good; it was the truth and it worked. I repeated my story in the other stores, and within a couple of hours I sold out my stock of one hundred ties at $1.00 each. My share was $50.00. I loved the wonderful feeling of independence. I went home elated at my success and fortune.

My father understood my excitement but said selling ties wasn't a dignified job for a young lady like me. I said, "What about your selling newspapers?" and he said, "You're right, dear, it's not very dignified and it's a temporary necessity, I hope, but I have other problems that you don't have. I don't have anyone to take care of me and my family. But you have me and Mother. Youth is not a career; it's a preparation, and you have a little more time to decide what you're going to do with your life. Sometimes it's better to take it a little slower." He said,

"You remember the Russian saying—you heard it all your life—
Tishe yedesh dolshe budish. The slower you travel the farther you
get."

I handed him the money I had earned, and that finished my
first career.

In the eighth grade I acquired a couple of friends of my own
age. Sarah lived a couple of blocks away. She was short, plump
and dark. Gertrude lived across the street from the candy store
in a three-story brown wooden house with a front porch. Her
mother was a widow and she had two older sisters and a
brother. (Despite all the progress and change in building in the
United States in the last fifty years, this particular short street,
Ditmas Avenue, between Second and Third Streets, had not
changed or improved at the time I went back in 1965 to take
pictures.) Gertrude's house was a mansion compared to the
hovel behind the candy store, or even the flat on the corner.

My father and mother worked from six in the morning until
eleven at night. When I came home from school I would relieve
Mother from three to six, so she could market and prepare
dinner. We never had a meal all together while Father had the
store. Usually she would prepare the meal, eat with the children, and put them to bed; then Father and I ate while she
minded the store . . . a dreary life for them.

I was able to have a little freedom at least two or three nights
after dinner, but there wasn't much I could do except go across
the street to Gertrude's or to the ice-cream parlor, or to a movie
once a week. That was after we had been here a year, and I was
enrolled in high school. The first year went fast while I crammed
and tried to learn English. It's miraculous how fast I got over
feeling like a mute. Rosalie and Lucy were terrific; in six months
they were speaking English like natives and had completely
blocked the Russian language from their memories.

Our routine was simple, out of necessity. Father got up at six;
our only bathroom was his to use first. By six fifteen he was
shaved, washed and ready for breakfast, which it was my duty
to prepare. Even in those two shabby rooms in back of the store I

made sure that everything on the table was sparkling clean. (I could never forget how fussy he was in Russia about the glass for his tea. He always held it up to the light to make sure that it sparkled.) Mother would join him for breakfast. They had to have that one meal alone, to have their privacy. The bathroom was then mine while they had their breakfast. By six forty-five they had finished, and would unpack the newspapers that had arrived in bundles during the night. These were sorted and arranged. The store was open for business. Then I had my breakfast. I used to fix it on a tray to eat in my own little corner while I did my homework and got ready for school. After I washed the breakfast dishes, I set the table for the next meal. Meanwhile Mother got Lucy and Rosalie washed and dressed. Rosalie was enrolled in public school, so Mother was able to tend the store with Lucy playing in the corner while we were off at school.

I guess I was a budding interior decorator in creating that little corner for myself in the middle of the family room that we used for the kitchen, living room and bedroom, and my first folding bed that was such a far cry from the many down perinas in Russia. Mother bought a couple of remnants of fabric. I made a throw for the wood crate that served as my table to match a bedspread that I handrolled to cover my bed, and I made myself a sausage bolster of the same fabric and stuffed it with straw so I could sit up in bed and study and have my breakfast on a tray next to me. My icon hung on the wall nearby, and I pretended I was the princess having breakfast in bed. But I couldn't get rid of the anxiety, the pain of feeling that I was on the outside looking in.

Father suggested that Joseph Barondess, our benefactor and guardian angel, whom I now called Uncle Joseph, was the logical one to call for advice on getting a summer job. He had come to see us a couple of times and we knew where he lived, not far away in Bensonhurst, but we had never been inside his house. I don't believe his wife and family shared his interest in the underprivileged. He had a wonderful personality and a shock of magnificent curly hair with a white streak in it. He reminded me very much of my paternal grandfather in both personality and appearance, except that Grandfather's features were more refined and he wore a beard. Joseph Barondess was a controversial union leader. Irving Howe, in his *World of Our Fathers*, describes him as "coarse and tender, commonplace and theatrical . . . the archetypal leader who grips the hearts of workers by mirroring in gaudy excess their yearnings for drama, storm, magnitude." I called him at his home and asked if I could see him for a few minutes for some advice. He told me he was taking the train to New York, and if I would meet him at the station, we would talk on the way.

On the train I told him abut my brief job selling ties, about my desire both to go back to school and to earn some money to lessen my father's burden. He told me that if I'd like to work in a bank during the summer vacation he would write a letter on my behalf to the manager of a bank on Delancey Street.

I took the note and got the job, at fifty dollars a month. I was to stand in the lobby by a table holding little dime savings banks, look pretty, smile, and ask every depositor coming by to buy a bank for ten cents apiece. I was still shy with my English and was conscious of a slight accent, but I didn't have much to say in this job. Everyone in the bank was perfectly lovely to me. They soon learned the story of the little girl who had been born in the United States, taken to Russia when she was six months old, and trapped by war, revolution, and horror. By the time the vacation was over, I was told that I could come back the following summer and have my job back.

Since the bank closed at three but the employees didn't leave until five p.m., I made myself useful in the bookkeeping department and other offices and ran errands for everybody. I was particularly fascinated by the Burroughs adding-machine operators. One of these women did it with lightning speed. Her proficiency fascinated me, and I asked her if she would show me how to operate it. She told me to come back at the end of the day when she was finished, which I did. She handed me a bunch of checks and I tried it. This job, I discovered, didn't need any English. I practiced every night for a month, and by the time I went back to school, I was pretty adept at the machine and had made up my mind that the following summer I would try to get a job as an operator.

The next step was Erasmus Hall High School. My I.Q. was much above average, and I had a record as a non-matriculated student who learned fast. My grades were excellent, except in spelling. Double vowels and double consonants throw me to this day. I made up, however, in other subjects.

The year was 1923. I was sixteen and flappers were in style. Although my life now was certainly a little more normal for my age, I still felt I was on the outside. Gertrude had red hair and fine perfect skin. Sarah was plump and short, pretty, and very dark. Gertrude's brother Edward used to invite his college friends to parties in their playroom. They played records, danced, and sang. When I was invited, I felt terribly shy. I met a boy there named Weil. Strange, I don't remember his first name, but I still remember Weil. He asked me to dance, and I felt awkward and speechless. He said, "What's the matter with you? Haven't you got a tongue?" I felt myself blush as I stammered, "I don't speak English very well." He burst out laughing. I felt as I had the day the kids called me "big dope." With a lump in my throat, I fled the house. Gertrude and Edward came after me, but I refused to go back. That night I determined that I would speak English better than Weil could. (Six years later, when I had my first ingenue role on Broadway, Weil came backstage to see me. I was speaking English well and playing an American girl. I reminded him of the incident and thanked him for laughing in my face. It was his turn to stammer and sound like a hick.)

In the fall of 1923, Stanislavsky's Moscow Art Theatre was in New York. Their repertory included Chekhov's *Cherry Orchard*, Dostoyevsky's *Brothers Karamazov*, Gorki's *The Lower Depths*, and Tolstoy's *Tsar Feodor*. Father took me to two of the four. Richard Boleslavsky was Stanislavsky's assistant. I saw the beginning of the Acting Method.

The summer of 1924 I went back to work at the Public National Bank, this time at the branch at 25th Street and Fifth Avenue. I was a Burroughs adding-machine operator at a salary of $60.00 a month. I was 17 years old. I loved the 25th Street branch on my beloved Fifth Avenue. In the fall I went back to high school, but I didn't like it; they weren't teaching me fast enough. We moved again, this time to a two-family house a few blocks away.

There was a boy in school named David Scudin, who was the football captain and extremely handsome. Montgomery Flagg made a drawing of him which was used in an Arrow collar ad in a magazine. (Ten years later he was a floor walker at Macy's.) His pretty girl friend, Antoinette, was the belle of Erasmus. I don't remember ever saying two words to her. I'm sure she wasn't aware of my existence and I don't think he was either, until the day he suddenly saw me and talked to me. There was a school dance coming up in a week and nobody had invited me. He said, "Hello," and asked me whom I was going to the dance with. I replied that I didn't have anybody to go with, and to my surprise he said, "I'll take you." And so I sped on wings to tell my mother that I was going to the dance with the football hero of the high school.

I had already decided I was going alone if necessary. A week earlier I had told Mother I needed a party dress. I knew she hated to turn me down, and I said if she would buy the fabric, I would make it myself. She agreed that it was a wonderful idea and bought me a piece of a most beautiful sapphire-blue velvet and a white lace Bertha collar, which was then in fashion. When I came home and discovered the fabric on the table, my mother was still at the store. I was excited. I put the fabric on the floor and started to cut the dress that I had designed in my mind.

When Mother came in, she cried out in horror, "Why didn't you wait? Did you look over the material carefully? Where did you put the damage?" "What damage," I asked, for I hadn't looked it over. Sure enough, she'd gotten a remnant with a great hole in it, and I had cut the dress with the damage smack in the middle of the skirt.

She said, "Don't you remember I always told you to measure seven times before you cut once?" But I had to finish the dress. I assured her I would find some way to cover up the damage. I turned the front of the skirt around to the back. With three yards of satin, crimson ribbon that she bought to make a sash, I created a bow with streamers that covered the hole. When I finished the dress, Mother laughed with approval. She said, "You look like the American flag, but it's a pretty dress!"

After ten minutes at the dance I learned that David had had a fight with Antoinette and that was why he had invited me. After the first dance he made up with her and forgot me, but I didn't care, because every dance after that was taken by one of the other boys in school. It felt good to discover that I was not a wallflower.

Another realization I came to that night was that I had learned all I was ever going to learn at Erasmus. The time had come to march on. It was the middle of the semester, but I went back to the bank and asked for my job back. I decided to go to night school. New York University was the logical choice for courses in public speaking and advanced English. I worked all day and went to school at night.

My chances of going full time to college were nil. My parents could never have afforded it. I was definitely a misfit. In my country I was an immigrant, just as I was the little American while I was in Russia. I wanted so desperately to belong. Three and a half years in America and almost eighteen years old . . . Father said education was the key, but the only key I knew was to work and learn at the same time. Being a realist, I knew my chances of graduating like everybody else were slim. It was not just insecurity; my determination to speak English like an American and lose my accent was so great that I neglected my other subjects, and gave up even trying to make a school like Hunter College.

By the summer of 1925 I knew every depositor at the Public National Bank. My father had sold the candy store and paid everybody back. He went into the printing business, and had offices on the lower East Side. He made the down payment on a two-family house at 1870 East 55th Street in Brooklyn. It was a typical development; all the houses looked alike.

My parents suggested that I keep my earnings and spend them on my wardrobe. There was a wonderful little Italian dressmaker, Arcuri, near us and I went to her for my first made-to-order dress. I felt so grown up and happy and I had to have something sensational. From *Vanity Fair* I picked out a picture of a bright red dress with black fagoting and she made it for me. I bought myself a large black cartwheel of a straw hat and I felt like a young lady.

Father was working hard and getting very thin. Everything was for Mother and the children. In the summer he sent her to the mountains for two weeks and to the Rockaway for a similar period.

Just about that time there was a movie called *Sally, Irene and Mary* that starred Sally O'Neil, Joan Crawford, and Constance Bennett. Gertrude, Sarah and I went to see it together. We were enchanted. At the corner ice-cream parlor we agreed to become a threesome like the girls in the picture. Gertrude and Sarah decided to change their names to Gerry and Sally, which would be perfect with my name. We would become Gerry, Sally, and Mary. I insisted that I wanted to change my name, too. They said it was silly. "Your name is right to begin with." I said Mary was too sweet and wish-washy for me, and I wanted to be Barbara like Barbara LaMarr, . . . and have my father's initials. And that's how I became Barbara Barondess instead of Mary Barondess. I could never dream that nine years later I would be featured in a film, *Beggar's Holiday*, with Sally O'Neill.

Although Gerry, Sally and Barbara were a trio of eighteen-year-olds that discussed their dreams and ambitions, they never discussed sex and knew absolutely nothing about it. It was a subject that we all avoided. I had blocked Marina's rape from my mind. The only thing I did know was that a girl had to be pretty untouchable if she wanted to be a nice girl. And since I had no steady boy friends, it was no problem.

By the end of the summer I had gotten into the habit of taking over the savings teller's booth while he went to lunch, because I brought my own snack and used to study during my lunch hour in the bank. While I was at his window, Frank Russek, head of the fabulous Russek's department store, sometimes came in. The first time I waited on him, he was startled to find a young lady. I explained that I was just pinch-hitting. He asked me what I did the rest of the time, and I told him I was a Burroughs operator.

He was surprised that a young girl would be doing a job like that. I suppose he was caught up by my enthusiasm, because he said that if I ever wanted to change my job, he would be happy to give me one in his store. He said they paid salesgirls $18.00 a week. I said I wouldn't change my job for that, but if there was any chance for advancement, and if I could become a buyer, I might consider it. He suggested that I come to see him and I did. He thought that the best way would be to place me in a different department for a few weeks at a time until I learned something about each, and that way the departments would evaluate my work. There was nothing more I could learn at the bank, so I went to work at Russek's for $25.00 a week.

I went from department to department. After a few weeks in each, I would pester Mr. Russek to let me into another department. Waiting on customers was a cinch after I learned how to make out sales slips and returns and credits. I was impatient. From all the visits to Mr. Russek's office I became friendly with his personal secretary, and after a couple of months she asked me to go on a double date with her. She knew two nice college boys who had a car. We were to go to a dance at the Astor Hotel to celebrate the ground-breaking for the Paramount Theater. The party was being given by Paramount Pictures and one of the boys was Eugene, the son of Adolph Zukor. It sounded like fun, so I brought my blue dress to the office. After the store closed, we changed in the ladies' room and then met the boys at the Astor. Eugene was my first and last blind date.

When we arrived at the dance I was delighted to find that real live movie stars were going to be there. There was a movie being made at the Paramount Studios in Astoria called *A Kiss for Cinderella*. The star was Betty Bronson and the director was Herbert Brennan. My date introduced me to Mr. Brennan, who asked me if I'd like to play a bit part of a bridesmaid. They were to start shooting the following week and my salary would be $15.00 a day! This was unheard of, the most wonderful thing that had ever happened to me. The next day I told my good news to Mr. Russek, quit my job, and reported to Astoria studio wardrobe.

When I told Mother, she was out of her mind with fury. She disappproved of my highfalutin ideas and told me she didn't know why I didn't stick to a good job and marry a nice boy who would take care of me. I was moving too fast, and she didn't like the whole idea. Getting mixed up with the movies and those bums would ruin me. She lost her temper, and we had a terrible battle. I told her if she was satisfied to live that way, it was her business, that I wasn't and that I was going to leave home. I went off to pack my bag.

Father arrived in the nick of time as I was walking out toward the elevated. I had no idea where I was going. He stopped me. After I told him what Mother had said, in his usual calm way he tried to explain her fears. He said she was worried for me, and that I must see her side of it. Finally, he persuaded me to come back with him. He would sit down with both of us and explain to Mother that I was perfectly safe in any career I chose. He said, "You know that I believe that you can take care of yourself and that you would never do anything that could hurt you or shame us." He looked at me with his tired blue eyes, and I knew that if he told me something white was black I would believe him. We went home, and Mother never again criticized anything I wanted to do.

CHAPTER SEVEN

I Want To Be an Actress

IT TOOK only one week on the set of Paramount in Astoria. I got the "bug." I wanted to be an actress, like Barbara LaMarr, Agnes Ayers, Pola Negri. My job as a bridesmaid lasted for about four weeks, and by now I was certain that this business was a stepping-stone to a future. I was going to learn the name of just about every casting director and movie company in the east, and how to look for other movie jobs.

I also learned about the wolves who were ready to devour every young girl who came across their path. The passes were crude and always came with a promise of how much they could do for you. They came from the casting directors and assistant directors, from the small guys who had very little power and were giving themselves airs. To spar with them was no small feat, but I made up my mind that I would outsmart them. I learned that talking about the Russian Revolution, the shooting of my father, my bullet wound, and our narrow escape worked like a miracle. Although some of the men had been in the war, most of them had not come close to horror and violence. I usually began with a remark about how grateful I was to be back in my wonderful country, and to have the opportunity to study and become an actress. That would change the subject: the invitation to bed became an invitation to coffee, lunch, or dinner. I earned the respect of a lot of little, would-be obnoxious guys.

D. W. Griffith was about to make a picture, *Sorrows of Satan*, with Carole Dempster at Astoria. To get into that was my next project. Since I had started with a bit part, I could be registered as a bit player. That was a break, because if you started as an extra, you usually stayed an extra all your life. I got the job in the Griffith picture.

In the following three months I covered all the casting offices diligently and was cast in a picture with Belle Bennett, Ben Lyon, and Lois Moran. It was called *Reckless Lady* and was also made in Astoria, but not by Paramount. Belle Bennett was a fabulous woman. She had been in movies since 1912, and had just made her greatest hit in Henry King's picture *Stella Dallas* (1925). Secretly I compared my mother with the character of Stella Dallas. Belle Bennett took a liking to me and told me wonderful tales about Hollywood. She was kind and generous and interested in me and my background. She encouraged my ambition to become an actress. She had two sons, one adopted. Just before this picture started, her own son was killed in an automobile crash. I was proud to have her autographed photograph, with a lovely inscription that she gave me before she went back to Hollywood.

All the money I made went for studying, for clothes, and for my third passion, the movies. I became familiar with the popular screen faces of 1926—Rudolph Valentino, Wallace Reid, Richard Dix, Harold Lloyd, Mary Pickford, Lillian and Dorothy Gish, Beatrice Joy, Bebe Daniels, Mary Brian, Betty Bronson— and a clean-cut, handsome comedian named Douglas MacLean, who was called the Prince of Hollywood. Little did any of us dream that in three or four years the careers of most of those stars, old and young, would be shattered by an invention called Vitaphone.

Curiously, I seldom saw the movies that I was in. They might not be released until a year or more later; I never got billing in those bit parts; and often there wasn't much left of my role in the finished movie. My parents never saw me on the screen in the silent parts.

I studied singing and dancing at a studio in Carnegie Hall and took more conventional courses at the City College of New York.

I learned to ride horseback. I discovered the American live theater—*Charlot's Revue* with Gertrude Lawrence, *Sunny* with Marilyn Miller, and *White Cargo*.

Mother was increasingly worried about my finding a husband and settling down. She said I was fickle, and I guess I was. Usually, after one date with a young man, I was through with him. The minute he wanted to "neck," I lost interest. The promiscuous pawing, the lack of control, left me cold. If one of the boys had had the grace to be subtle or romantic, I'm sure I would have responded. But they all seemed so awkward and boorish that they repelled me. Perhaps my reading had made me an incurable romantic. My Prince Charming had to have dignity and poise, a brain, a heart, compassion, talent, and most of all sportsmanship and courage. Much of this I confided to my girlfriend, Gerry, my principal sounding board. We discussed our ideals freely, but sex was never mentioned.

In the spring of 1926, I had a small part in a picture called *All Aboard* being made in Steeplechase Park in Coney Island. The star was Johnny Hines. George Tilyou, owner of Steeplechase, allowed the motion picture company to use the park for location. We worked there several weeks, and Mr. Tilyou, a gentle and charming man with a slight limp, visited us on the set frequently.

Quite by accident, I discovered that I had acrophobia. I don't know whether I'd always had it or whether it was the result of an accident I'd been involved in a couple of months before. Some friends had suggested the "scenic railway"—the roller coaster—at Coney Island, which was a mile long and the highest one there. Near the end of the exciting ride, the track split under the car we were riding in. The impact hurled six people out, when we were almost a hundred feet from the ground. Three were badly injured; one was crippled; my friend broke a leg. I, with my usual luck, broke the fall with my hands and came out with a split lip and a few bruises. The lip, fortunately, healed quickly, though it left a tiny scar that I still have. Naturally, this picture was about an amusement park, and in it we had to ride the loop-the-loop. I was terrified of getting into the car, but my desire to be a pro was so great that I gritted my teeth and went on with the show.

Mr. Tilyou threw a party for the cast and gave us all season passes to the park. Although I disliked the crowded beaches and hated Coney Island, I loved swimming. That pass was soon to play, as they say, an important part in my life.

Right after we finished the Hines picture, I went on my first location to Connecticut. The picture was called *The Girl on the Barge*. The star was Sally O'Neil, pretty little Sally from *Sally, Irene and Mary*. Edgar McGregor was the leading man. The character lead was Jean Hersholt and there was a child actress, Nancy Kelly. The director from Hollywood was Edward Sloman.

The cast of a picture, I learned, is not like that of a play. Sometimes you can have an important part in a picture and never meet any of the cast except the people you're directly involved with. But on location, in pictures, people get to know each other fairly well. Although this was my first time away from home, I did not feel lonely. I realized in my aloneness that self-reliance was part of the price.

A few weeks after that, another director arrived from Hollywood to make a picture. I had another small bit, and the director and I became good friends. He was French, had come to this country just a few years before with his parents and two brothers, so we had that experience in common. He came to New York several times during the next few years and we would go out to dine and dance. I found him sensitive and brilliant. He told me that his cousin was Carl Laemmle, head of Universal Studio, where he was working. I had a feeling that he felt like a poor relation and, although I never told him, the thought bound me to him with affection. He wasn't an important director and he told me how dissatisfied he was with the "B" and "C" pictures he was assigned to. I had a premonition that this man had a tremendous, bottled-up talent that would burst forth if he ever got the proper chance. I never wavered in my opinion, and I'm glad to say that I was perfectly right. He became one of the directorial giants of the movie business. His name is William Wyler.

Just before finishing the picture with Wyler, the company planned a birthday party for him. Willy's birthday was July first. When I mentioned that mine was the fourth, they decided to make it a joint party. It was my first birthday party since 1916. In the ten years I had forgotten what birthday parties were like. I was toasted, everybody gave me a present, and I was ecstatic when we said goodbye. I went home right after my nineteenth birthday. In many ways I felt one hundred and five. On my return home, I regaled Gerry—she was my most avid audience by now—with tales of the talented, wonderful exciting people I had met.

I didn't have another picture scheduled until August 5— *Summer Bachelors*—for the Fox Studio in New York. It was to be directed by Allan Dwan and Mat Moore and a new actress, Leila Hyams, playing her first lead. On August 4, I remembered my pass to Steeplechase Park and told Gerry that since they had that marvelous big swimming pool we ought to go there. I knew I wasn't going to see anybody I knew, so I chose my oldest bathing suit, a striped one that Mother had bought me the year before. Her taste wasn't the best; the stripes ran the wrong way, horizontally, and I didn't like it. But I decided to save my good one. My hair was quite long and light chestnut brown. Since I had never found a bathing cap that would keep it dry, I usually swam without a cap.

We were having a wonderful time splashing and racing when Gerry pointed in the direction of a short little man trying to get my attention at the side of the pool. I swam over, my hair sopping wet. He said in a terribly annoyed voice, "That's a pretty stupid thing to do, getting all messy and wet."

I was astonished—he was pretty fresh! Holding to the edge of the pool, I said, "Are you trying to be funny? I have a pass to come here and to swim, and I'm swimming."

He said, "You dames drive me crazy. Do you think this is the way to be in a contest? How do you think you're going to look?"

I said, "What are you talking about?"

He glared at me as if I were out of my mind. By now Gerry had reached me and was listening to the conversation. I didn't know about a contest and I wished he would leave me alone.

He must have realized I was telling the truth. His tone of voice changed. "Please, get out of the pool. I would like to have a talk with you." Gerry nudged me and said, "Come on, let's see what this is all about." I climbed out. The man appraised me from the top of my dripping head to the tip of my toes, and said, "If you don't know what I'm talking about, I apologize. If you don't know about the contest, I'll tell you about it, but we haven't got much time. If you're not in it, you should be. I have seen the girls, and even with your lousy bathing suit you'll walk away with the first prize." I said, "What prize?" He said, "One thousand bucks and the title of Miss Greater New York."

I thought I would make a fool of myself in that suit and with my hair all wet. The contest was due to go on in ten minutes.

Gerry said, "Come on, Barbara, it's exciting. Be a sport; this is fun—nobody'll know if you don't win."

Another challenge. I don't think it took longer than thirty seconds to convince me. Gerry handed me a lipstick and a comb, but my hair was too wet to do any good, and we hurried to where the contest was being held. Earl Carroll was one of the judges, and Raoul Walsh, the movie director, was another. I got into the line, and someone hung a number four on my arm. Gerry stood a few feet away and waved.

The line consisted of about seventy-five girls. I was too excited to look at any of them. I didn't know what they looked like until I saw their faces in the paper the next day. It was a strange experience to parade back and forth as the judges called out the numbers of the girls to be eliminated. Every time they called a number I was sure the next would be number four. When there were only five of us left, I was positive I would be eliminated next.

Suddenly I looked, and there were only three of us left. Oh, my God, I thought, I'll win the third prize. It wasn't me. They announced the second prize. It wasn't me. And then I heard, "First prize, Number Four," and I was frozen. They asked me to step forward.

I thought they must be crazy. It can't be true; I must be dreaming. In a second I was surrounded by judges and someone was pinning a ribbon across my chest. I was handed an enormous silver cup and a check, and the Fox News camera started to grind.

Everybody was smiling and congratulating me. I felt as if I'd been caught naked on Forty-Second and Broadway: the flashbulbs were going off, newspaper men were photographing me. As I saw Gerry's delirious face, I realized I wasn't dreaming.

I learned later that until that year the contest had been spiked with professional beauties and show girls from such extravaganzas as Earl Carroll's *Vanities*. Somebody had exposed the fact that last year's winner was not an amateur as had been claimed. That was why my competition was not much of a challenge. Maybe my little bits in four silent movies would have disqualified me too—I don't know. No one asked me what I did. All I gave the little man was my name. Gerry filled in the address and miscellaneous information while I was parading in front of the judges.

When we finally got home, I was still in a daze. A reporter was already at the house to interview and take pictures of Mother and the kids, who didn't know anything about the contest, naturally. When the newsman first arrived, Mother had been frightened, thinking I had done something scandalous. It was wonderful and horrible.

That was August 4, 1926. The next morning, I was due at Fox Studio, so I got onto the subway with the morning papers and my makeup box. I got a seat and opened the paper. The headlines read "Miss Greater New York, Modern Venus, 1926." I still didn't believe it. I sneaked a look at the other people settled down with their newspapers, and noticed a couple of them looking at me and then back at the paper with a sort of double take. A couple of people across the aisle nudged each other and smiled at me. Before we reached Times Square, I didn't know whether to smile or pretend not to know what they were looking at, so I just suffered self-consciously until I could get off.

I checked into the studio on Eighth Avenue and went straight to the makeup department. While I was having my makeup put on, the Fox publicity man came in with the paper in his hand. He said, "Miss Barondess, as soon as you are through, I'd like to take you over and introduce you to Mr. Dwan, the director. This is a marvelous break for the picture and you, and we should take advantage of the Modern Venus in our midst."

While I was finishing my makeup, I couldn't help but think, first I was pointed at because I was living in Russia and born in America; then I was pointed at in America because I'd come from Russia; and now I'm being pointed at because I'm a beauty contest winner. I do want to be an actress, so I'm going to have to get used to being pointed at. I guess being good copy isn't so bad. The only trouble is that you must never let yourself be caught in the wrong situation. I've made my choice to live in a fish bowl. And I'll have to learn how to cope with it.

Of course, everyone made a fuss, and Mr. Dwan decided to enlarge my part. In the next few days the following item appeared in one of the papers:

> Miss Barbara Barondess, of Fox Company, just won the Modern Venus Contest at Steeplechase Park in Coney Island.

I became in spirit, but not literally, one of the company. But I still didn't feel secure. I was happy about the contest, but the prize money was the only reality, along with the silver cup. Another article said:

Barbara Barondess of Brooklyn has won the Modern Venus Contest and has accepted the offer of a large movie producer to appear in films. She is to appear in stellar roles.

This should have made me happy, but it didn't. I knew it was far from the truth. For the studio, it was a way to get the picture mentioned in the paper, and for me, perhaps, to get my name a little better known. They were using me and I had to use them.

Being a realist, I knew that winning the contest was a fluke, and when I read another article a few days later, I knew they were going to milk this publicity all they could, and as soon as I got to be yesterday's news I'd be out of luck unless I made some move in another direction.

I haven't said enough about my mother. I'm conscious that it was my father who motivated my life. As I go back through the past, through the cluttered attic of my mind, I see that what seemed devastatingly important when it happened was really not very important. I've never undergone psychoanalysis, but now, as I dig into the past, I feel that that's what it must be like, a purge of the soul. And I can only remember what I thought, not what I felt. It's almost impossible to recapture pain or joy; time seems to dull it.

Mother was extremely beautiful when we arrived in this country, and she was in her early thirties. She was, after all, only twenty years older than I. My growing up so fast distressed her, and she was disturbed at my eagerness to tell my age. Her fear of growing old was strong, and perhaps subconsciously I resented the fact that my father was aging faster than she was. To me she seemed vain and empty-headed. She had a terrible temper. She was interested only in having a good time. She had a sweet soprano voice and loved to sing and dance and swim. I can see now that she was frustrated and undisciplined. In the first ten years that we were in this country, she gained about forty pounds, and reached about 160. I begged her to diet but it did no good. She was under five feet two and was fat until she died at the age of seventy-seven, but that didn't stop her from singing and dancing until the last week of her life.

I wondered if she loved her children. I don't remember any fond or loving gesture from her toward any of us—nothing like my father's hugs and warmth and patient reasoning and teaching. I associate all the affection and fun with him. He took me to the circus and to my first museum, brought me my first books and taught me many things about life in general.

I think one of the reasons that my mother never had a birthday party for me even after it was possible was that she dreaded to see the candles on the cake. That thought has stayed with me my whole life, and on my fiftieth birthday I insisted on all the candles. My husband, whose sense of humor was caustic, said it looked like a great forest fire. My friends, of course, laughed it off and said that I looked much younger. My answer was that I'd rather be a good fifty than a tired twenty-eight.

In the following months I was busy and had several small parts in pictures I have forgotten. My name was mentioned often in the newspapers, and I enjoyed being temporarily a "celebrity." My mother was disturbed by my ambition and didn't know how to handle me. I spent little time in Brooklyn and felt alien to that neighborhood, even to the friends of the last four years. They were beginning to treat me with diffidence. They were fascinated, but to them I became a little strange. Our home looked shabby and dull to me. I knew it was the best Father could do for us, and I was happy that at least I was not being a burden financially, but I felt more than ever that we lived on the wrong side of the tracks. I lost my roots.

As the winner of the contest I was eligible to compete for the title of Miss America in Atlantic City. Some of my movie acquaintances thought I should be thrilled at this great chance for more publicity, but I wasn't. The contests in those days were not organized the way they are today, with the intense promotion and elaborate tours. Unless a girl did a lot of self-promotion, in a couple of months it was all forgotten. I wasn't sure that the movies were my medium and I thought that perhaps the stage was. I couldn't compete for the title of Miss America unless I was willing to give up the movies until after the contest, and secretly I never believed that Miss Greater New York had a chance to become Miss America, so I withdrew and went on trying to learn to act for the stage.

CHAPTER EIGHT

Broadway

O NE SUNDAY about a month after the contest I went to Long
Beach with some friends, and while we were lying on the
sand two men, one rather plump and thick in the middle, the
other very skinny, dapper and with a mustache, walked over,
introduced themselves, and told me they were theatrical agents.
The plump one was Louis Shurr; his skinny partner was Harry
Bestry. Shurr's specialty was musical comedy; Bestry's was the
legitimate theater. They recognized who I was, and Bestry
handed me his card and said, "If you want to go into show
business, come and see me."

I had heard about Shurr. New York show people knew him as
the man who owned a beautiful lady's coat of Russian white
ermine. He loaned it to every date he took out to a theater
opening or restaurant. At all the big events you could always
spot Shurr, with a different girl every time wearing the same
glamorous coat.

Bright and early the next day I was in their office, where they
went over the list of shows being cast, and Mr. Shurr personally
escorted me to a theater where auditions were being held for a
Shubert production. I had on a new, black princess-style dress

97

with a red fox border and black cloche hat. I felt like a movie star—until I stepped into the theater.

I had never been back stage in a theater except to see a performance. The empty stage, a dark hole, startled and oppressed me. The single work light looked lonely. The stage manager sat at a small desk on stage. There were a few people milling around and a half dozen people sitting in the audience section, talking to each other and paying no attention to the auditions. The people on stage looked small; the theater looked cold, bleak, and unglamorous.

I was instructed to walk onto the stage, which was slowly filling up with other girls who had come in the side door. I hadn't the slightest idea who the star was, or the name of the play or the producer. The stage manager asked the girls to line up, just as in the beauty contest.

Someone in the theater occasionally called to one of the girls to step aside. Obviously some of them were known by name, and when the owner of the mysterious voice didn't know the name he would say, "Third from the left," or "The girl in the red dress," or whatever designation came into his head.

Evidently Louis Shurr had told him my name, because I heard, "Miss Barondess, please step out and register at the stage manager's desk." Out of about eighty girls who showed up, approximately twenty were chosen.

When the others left, two men came up from the audience onto the stage. One was a small, heavy-set man with a pot belly—J. J. Shubert. The other one, with a rakish hat, was Al Jolson. And that's when they announced that this was to be a road show of *Artists and Models*, an Al Jolson musical. Louis Shurr disappeared.

I told Messrs. Shubert and Jolson that I did not intend to start my career as a showgirl, and I would not go on the road. I suppose Mr. Shubert was amused by my candor and nerve. He told me to come to his office and he'd put me in a New York show. At last—Broadway! I became a junior member of Actors

Equity and my salary was $75.00 per week, a come down, but steady . . . if it was a hit.

A few days later the following item appeared in a newspaper:

Prize Beauty for *Gay Paree*. Winner of a recent American Venus Contest at Coney Island will appear in the new *Gay Paree* which will be presented in New York soon. Miss Barondess is to appear in a number of spectacular scenes in the new revue. She entered the American [sic] Venus Contest in Coney Island recently in the spirit of fun. The judges of the 172 contestants declared that her figure most nearly resembled the Venus de Milo. She has received many stage offers. She chose *Gay Paree*.

The cast consisted of Winnie Lightner, Charles (Chick) Sale, Richard Bold, Al Wohlman, Max Hoffman, Jr., Barbara Barondess, Alice Bolden, Frank Gabby, Jack Haley, Benny Rubin, and Jeanne Aubert, a glamorous French singer. I was in the prologue and two sketches. In addition I pitched in with five other girls in the three spectacular showgirl numbers. All we had to do in those numbers was walk, strut, and pose in elaborate costumes. During rehearsals I was given the opportunity to understudy some of the principals. After four weeks of rehearsal, we were to open in New Haven, then Philadelphia.

During our New Haven opening, the great Dempsey-Tunney fight was being broadcast on the radio, and I was so excited listening to it in the wings that I missed a cue, an unpardonable sin in the theater. The tough stage manager, Zeke Caldwin, never forgave me.

Gay Paree was the beginning of my education in the ways of ambitious showgirls, in the coarse and raucous backstage life that has been the subject of many plays and movies. It didn't matter whether these "gals" came from the heart of New York City or Timbuktu—their world narrowed down to the blocks on either side of Broadway from 42nd Street to 52nd Street. Their principal interest was who was sleeping with whom, who got a fur coat or a piece of jewelry, and how long the show was going to run.

These girls hung out together in the coffee shops, often lived together, and seemed to know everything about each other, and about producers, directors, stage managers, and other theater men who made their lives interesting. They knew about these men's private sex lives, which stars or chorus girls were the current favorites of the VIPs—some liaisons that were in the gossip columns and many that were kept from the public.

Jeanne Aubert was a willowy blonde who did a couple of numbers in French and was billed as an important star. She created a lot of excitement backstage because she would arrive in a Rolls-Royce, with a personal maid. She had a magnificent wardrobe, including the inevitable furs and jewelry—all thanks to a Chicago tycoon who was crazy about her. He brought her a gift every day. Before each performance the girls would gather in her dressing room and see the latest Token of Esteem, usually from Tiffany or Cartier.

It was when Mlle. Aubert showed us her solid gold hairpins that I decided I had had enough of musical-comedy life. I was already bored. The publicity was nice, but Rolls-Royces and gold hairpins! I had a different idea of what a stage career should be and I decided to look for a part in a dramatic play, after about a month in New York. Besides, Seymour Felix, the dance director, discovered that I couldn't dance.

Gay Paree opened at the Winter Garden on October 28, 1926, and was a hit. I wanted to understudy in the show, so Winnie Lightner took me under her wing. I tagged along with her to song publishing firms in Tin Pan Alley and she taught me how to put over a song. The first day I went with her I met Jimmy McHugh, and he taught me how to sing "I Can't Give You Anything But Love, Baby." So I found another outlet for my restless energy. I never got to go on for Miss Lightner, however.

My subscription to *Variety* made me familiar with the names of every casting director, producer, and agent in New York. I made my rounds every day; Shubert Alley and Tin Pan Alley became my familiar beat. When I wasn't looking for a job, I was learning to sing. In those days the composers hung around their publishing houses to plug their own work and teach young singers their songs. One of the songwriters I met was Lou Alter, who taught me his "My Kind of Love." Abner Silver, who had a couple of current popular songs when I met him, said, "You're so pretty, I could write a song about you." I giggled and said, "You tell that to all the girls." But he said, "I really can; now listen to this." And he started to hum and improvise a strain on the piano. While he was doing this, a short, dark man stuck his head into the office door and Abner said, "Billy, come help me with this project. She doesn't believe I can write a song for her." Billy Rose, who looked like a racetrack tout, laughed and stayed for about a half hour while they knocked out a song called "Barbara." No smash hit, but I was thrilled when it was recorded by Ben Bernie and published by Harms with a dedication to me on the top sheet.

I was still in *Gay Paree* when I was offered a straight part in a play called *The Spider* by Fulton Oursler. I didn't want to leave *Gay Paree* yet, because with a new play you could rehearse for a week and be fired, and I wanted to be sure I had another job before I gave notice. At that time New York rehearsals lasted four to six weeks. While playing in *Gay Paree* and rehearsing *The Spider,* Al Woods told me about a new play called *Crime* by Sam Shipman. It would give me an opportunity to play two separate parts, one in the second act and one in the third. The first part was as a black girl, a decoy for jewel robbers. It was a scene in front of a jewelry store with her boyfriend, played by Jack LaRue—also his first chance. In the third act, I would play a night-club singer doing a parody on Peaches Browning's "Romance of the Day."

Going from blackface to singing appealed to me. I quit both *The Spider* and *Gay Paree* and took a chance that I wouldn't be fired from *Crime.* James Rennie, Kay Johnson, and Chester Morris were the stars; the juvenile leads were played by a young actor from Pasadena, Douglass S. Montgomery, and Sylvia Sidney.

Sylvia Sidney, who had a previous hit in *The Squall* with Blanche Yurka, was playing her first ingenue lead, and I became her understudy in *Crime.* Kay Johnson and Chester Morris had been the stars of *Desire Under the Elms* the year before. James Rennie was a movie idol and the husband of Dorothy Gish. Douglass Montgomery and Jack LaRue were making their debut on Broadway—and Kay Francis was playing a small bit.

Sylvia's mother was around a lot. She was a very energetic, small woman, who hovered in protection of her daughter. I didn't know the term "stage mother" but I always thought of her as a cackling hen.

We usually ate at Billy Lahiff's "Tavern" on West 48th Street during our rehearsal breaks. It was a favorite with theater people, and Bill Lahiff, a jovial man, had pictures of his niece all around the restaurant. Nancy Carroll was a real movie star. Sylvia moved fast to stardom on Broadway. She was in a half dozen plays in four years. With her youth, beauty and talent, she was a natural for Hollywood and movie fame. Sylvia had a lovely, heart-shaped face, and was a small girl, about five feet one inch, with the kind of full bust that would have been in style and an asset ten years later. But in 1929 being flat chested was the fashion, and the poor girls who were well endowed went through hell strapping themselves down and dieting in the hope that they would lose there too. That didn't happen. Sylvia was a pretty, sophisticated girl by seventeen and had a very good idea where she was going. I was impressed with her.

One small part in the first act was played by Kay Francis. She was a very tall, striking girl, with a small head and tiny feet. She carried herself with an air of confidence that gave the impression of haughtiness. In all the weeks of rehearsal and tryouts in New Haven and Philadelphia we never spoke. She behaved like a snobbish loner. I didn't learn until a few years later that she was always getting over a perpetual hangover. Most of the others in the cast were warm and friendly, particularly the young ones starting out.

So I entered the fascinating world of the legitimate theater in January of 1927. During the tryouts in Philadelphia there was a disagreement with the director and he was replaced by Guthrie McClintic, who rarely directed anything other than plays for his wife, Katharine Cornell. Mr. McClintic scarcely said a word to me. I went through my lines never knowing whether he thought I was hopeless or so richly talented that I didn't need direction. But I never missed a word he said to anyone. During the run of *Gay Paree* in Philadelphia, Boston, and the Winter Garden in New York, I received a complete sex education from the cast. When they found out that I was a virgin they took me under their wing to describe every trick they knew and the pitfalls. Mostly, they were a tough and sad lot. The only other novice to show business was a beautiful redhead who became my best friend. Her name was Lenore Wilder. We saw a great deal of each other for years until geography separated us. The Broadway producers mostly were a crude lot. To sort them out and work out a strategy of self protection and survival took careful planning and research. But it was worth the effort because it worked like a charm, and I never had to reject their attention and chance the wounding of their egos by saying no. They weren't all crude. There were exceptions. But there were enough of them that were impossible. J. J. Shubert was so tied up with his mistress and her three or four sisters who were all employed in the various box offices and kept their eyes open and spied on everything that he did that we joked about his mistress watching him like a hawk. He couldn't even go to the men's room without her. He was short and roly-poly with a big pot belly. His mistress was a very attractive, hefty blonde, about one foot taller than he. Lee Shubert was skinny, like a sailor boy. His face was almost black from continuous sunlamp treatment. He had beady black eyes, was impeccably dressed, rarely smiled, and made absolutely no small talk. He was called "the sphinx" or "the Indian." His version of a pass was to push a girl against the wall as she walked through his office. The first time I called on him was late morning, just before lunch. As I walked into his office, the door closed behind me. Before he even asked my name, I was startled by a move that pushed me right against the wall. I was speechless, but not for long. It happened to be my lucky day. I was in my menstrual period (this was before Tampax was invented). I was well padded with double sanitary napkins. The moment he shoved against me, he jumped back as if he had been burnt. In that split second was born the strategy that I used very successfully afterward. I was so taken aback by his crude, unexpected attack that I made no sound of rejection—only surprise. I smiled sweetly and said, "Sorry, wrong time." To cover his embarrassment, he asked me my name, and I made sure that he learned I was a Barondess. I called on several producers that day, and the next, and found out a lot about the ones I called on. Gilbert Miller was married to a Wall Street heiress, Kitty. He was very social, and elegant in speech and manner, but somewhat sloppy in appearance. He made me feel that he wanted to make a pass, but there was too much at stake with his wife's money. Lucky for me. Al Woods, the first producer I met through Joseph Barondess, treated me like a niece. He was a big, flabby man with one injured eye who knew the Barondess name stood for a good, solid, family background. Al Lewis, the producer of *The Jazz Singer*, was a nice, little family man who didn't fool around. I discovered that the Jewish producers mostly fooled around Christian girls and married the Jewish ones, and the Christian producers married Christian girls and tried to fool around with the Jewish ones. Of course, there are always exceptions and there were some successful mixed marriages. I went to see the pushovers once a month, usually fortified with sanitary napkins—whether I needed them or not. It limited my visits to once every three and a half weeks, but they never forgot me. Ziegfeld had a reputation for generosity . . . like diamond bracelets for the girls he liked. His approach was a little subtler than the other bulls. But I didn't take any chances. With every new producer, I was fortified—just in case. My first call on Mr. Ziegfeld was a pleasant surprise. He didn't make a pass and offered me a job in *Rio Rita*. Old William Brady was a big man, about six feet two or three inches, with a heavy gold chain across his middle, who looked like he slept in his clothes. He reeked of liquor. He had a terrible reputation, but by the time I met him, I was an established actress and wrote a column for the *Morning Telegraph*. Strangely enough, that little column printed five days a week gave me a status that everybody respected. As a serious student, I carried a briefcase with a sketch pad and a book. I made sure to make every producer feel that I respected his opinion and appreciated his advice, on any subject I could think of. I asked them what I should study, whom I should see, how I should implement my desire to become a fine actress, and so on. It made them feel strong, superior, macho and worked like a charm for a while.

Crime was a hit, but after about six weeks in New York I became restless again. By this time I had learned all the facts of life backstage. Virtue was only a matter of time as far as show business was concerned, and morality was unknown. But for me it was a matter of principle. I was not going to be used like a paper towel. I was determined to become proficient enough to earn a place by craft and talent. I was sure that I would meet my Prince some day and have romance and love, and marry and have children and live happily ever after.

S. N. Behrman, the fine playwright whose then current hit was *The Second Man*, became a friend. He and Kenyon Nicholson, author of *The Barker*, spent many afternoons buying me coffee and listening to my hopes and ambitions. I met writers, directors and actors. I was dedicated to becoming an actress. Barrie, as Sam Behrman was called, used to kid me about my puritanical ideas. I suppose they thought the kid from Brooklyn via Russia was amusing. As I look back I wonder if they were laughing at me or with me. At any rate, they listened. My usual routine was to come to Manhattan about noon; call on agents and producers; go to Momma and Poppa Vincent Sardi's newly opened restaurant for lunch (if I had the 85 cents); see my friends in the afternoon; job-hunt some more; and report to the theater when I was working. Our hangouts were the Hotel Astor lobby, Sardi's and Walgreen's Drug Store. Sardi's is the only one that is still there.

One of the producers, Horace Liveright, whom I called on was also a publisher. He had produced the original *Dracula* running on Broadway at the time, and *The Firebird*. He was attractive in a strange way and produced Patrick Kearney's adaptation of *An American Tragedy* by Theodore Dreiser. Prematurely gray, Liveright must have been in his middle or late thirties. I thought of him as an older man, much more educated and intellectual than the average producer I had met, and of course I was flattered when he invited me to go with him to a party.

The hostess—very large, very wealthy, with an enormous apartment—was a patron of the opera; her fat, ugly daughter was studying voice. Her huge parties were famous, and her guests were famous or rich or both. Miss Greater New York or not, I felt like a lucky mouse on the outside looking in. At that party I met Otto Kahn, the great banker, also a patron of the opera. He was very short, white-haired, with beautiful, graceful hands, but it was his unusual eyes that fascinated me. They were amber colored, with a dark gray rim around the iris. Those eyes were so haunting that I wished I could draw a picture of his face and I did. I also became friendly with Irving Hoffman, an artist who was only about eighteen but doing wonderful caricatures of theater people for the newspapers. Irving was a tall, skinny kid with thick eyeglasses, and a wonderful kind heart and sense of humor and very shy.

Through Horace and Irving I met all the young talents of the day that were original and emerging to great recognition—Peter Arno, Lois Long, and many of the newspaper men—some whom I went out with and some whom I just met around. Robert Coleman, the critic on the *Mirror*, took me to opening nights when I was not working. I met Hoffman's parents and

younger brother. They were a close, loving family and in constant fear that Irving would lose his sight. He was terribly near-
sighted. Because of this he was a self-conscious young man who
pretended to be a sophisticated cynic. Of course I saw right
through him and knew him as a sensitive, talented and most
generous young man. I knew he sold many caricatures without
telling his mother, so he could give money to actors and writers
who were out of work.

Through Irving I met Walter Winchell, Sidney Skolsky, most
of the then current theater critics, and a French artist, Marcel
Morel, at whose study I met Harry Sternberg, who taught at the
Art Students League. I was fascinated at Marcel's studio, which
Irving and Harry often used, to watch the deftness of the three
artists at work. Marcel was gaining a reputation for lithographs
and drawings of stars like Katharine Cornell, and I was inspired
to draw and paint.

The boys thought this a marvelous idea. Irving gave me a
book on anatomy that I still own, and Marcel, lessons in drawing. Marcel, with his delicious French accent, named us the
Three Musketeers and the Girl. We had a lot of fun, and after a
couple of weeks of drawing I did a sketch of Otto Kahn's face
from memory. The boys complimented me and suggested that I
call Kahn and show it to him. I was so pleased that I did exactly
that.

Mr. Kahn remembered me and invited me to tea. When I got
to his house on Fifth Avenue and found myself in front of a
magnificent mansion, I couldn't help thinking that Warsaw was
not so far away. Although things didn't seem at the time to be
happening fast enough for me, an awful lot had happened in the
years since I was in America. A butler led me into an impressive
foyer. When Mr. Kahn came out to greet me, he seemed even
smaller in contrast to the enormous ceilings and the magnificent
opulence of the place. He led me into the library, where I
showed him my sketch. He liked it very much and asked if I
wanted to be an artist. I said no, I wanted to be an actress. He

asked me a lot of questions and spent about an hour with me while we were served tea. He, too, was interested to hear about our escape from Russia. He told me that if I ever changed my mind about acting and wanted to become an artist he would be happy to subsidize me and send me to Paris to study art.

I was flabbergasted. I never dreamed that I had any talent in that direction. For me, drawing was a pleasant pastime. The thought of drawing anything that would be of use or pleasure to anybody else hadn't entered my mind. I was oblivious to anything else; my own little one-track mind wanted me to become an actress. Before I left, Mr. Kahn gave me a little package. Perhaps he had a drawer full of them and gave them away as souvenirs, but to me whatever was inside was a treasure, the first present I had ever received from a stranger. He handed it to me as I left, saying, "A little souvenir for good luck. I'm sure you'll go far in whatever career you choose, and this is to remind you that you have plenty of time." I stammered my thanks and left. I walked down Fifth Avenue to 63rd Street and sat down on the same bench at the zoo entrance where Father had sat with me four years before. I thought, how strange that Mr. Kahn had said the same thing my father always said, that I had plenty of time. I opened my little package and in it was an oblong silver box, the size of a small matchbox. The top slid open, and in it was an exquisite traveling watch.

I don't know how long I sat on my bench at 63rd Street. The business rush was over, and dusk was pulling its protective shawl over the city. I remember it as a most beautiful evening. I suppose even if it weren't, I would remember it that way. Lights were flickering on in the tall buildings like fireflies. My city! The most beautiful city in the world. I recalled every word Father had said, and I remembered my tears. I closed my eyes and could almost hear his whisper: "Expect the best of everything, but remember to make the best of everything you get." I looked up 63rd Street, my chosen street, and thought, God has been good to me. My father is right. Some day I will live in one of those houses.

Six months on Broadway was considered a hit, and once *Crime* attained this status, my restlessness got the best of me. I got a radio show on a station owned by Donald Flamm, WPCH. It was a fifteen-minute daily routine. I read poetry (Edna St. Vincent Millay, Dorothy Parker, Samuel Hoffenstein) and sang songs to piano accompaniment ("The Man I Love," "No Wonder I'm Blue," "Stormy Weather," "My Man," mostly the popular "torch songs" of the day). I was going on with my attempt to learn to put over a song and played every benefit or anything that would give me experience and competence. I became friendly with two young agents from the William Morris office—Michael Meyerberg, who later became an important producer (*Candide, Skin of Our Teeth, Waiting for Godot, Lute Song*, etc.) and Johnny Hyde, who later became one of the heads of the William Morris office. (He is credited with discovering Marilyn Monroe, with whom he was deeply in love.) I had a repertoire of many torch songs, with special arrangements made for me by Lou Alter, George Gershwin, Vernon Duke—anybody I could get to transpose the songs to suit my low vocal range. George said I sang "between the cracks," but when I told him I wanted to sing "The Man I Love," he transposed it and rehearsed me in it.

Michael and Johnny booked me into a second-rate vaudeville house in New York on 125th Street. I was the last-minute replacement for somebody who couldn't make it. They said it was only a second spot, which was considered probably the worst on the vaudeville bill, but they thought it important for me to stand up in front of an audience and get the experience and exposure. Frozen with fear, I asked George Gershwin whether he thought I should do it. He thought it a good idea, and went over the songs with me. I told him that no one could play for me the way he did, and I didn't know if I could explain to the theater orchestra the tempo of my peculiar half-talking, half-singing, so he magnanimously suggested that he would play the first performance, and show the orchestra how to accompany me. I was delirious with joy.

This was to be our secret. All I was to do when I got to the theater was tell the manager that I had brought my own pianist for the first show. I must have done fairly well with his support because after the show the manager came to tell me how pleased he was. George was there, saying goodbye and telling me that the orchestra was instructed, not to worry, that everything would go all right. When I introduced the manager to George, he practically screamed, "My God, you should have told me before! I would have put his name in front instead of yours." George laughed, but after he left the orchestra every performer treated me with profound respect.

George was a good friend, and I enjoyed his company the few moments that we ever spent alone, but it was not very often. Most of the time he was surrounded by people. I think he could have written music if he were sitting in the middle of 42nd Street and Broadway. He had a capacity for removing himself from his physical surroundings to a level where his brain heard all those beautiful sounds that he put on paper for the world to hear.

I remember one of the first large parties he took me to. He never had to be asked to play a piano; if there was one in the room he gravitated to it as if a magnet were pulling him. That night he sat at the piano and played. After a couple of hours I looked around and realized I didn't know a soul in the room. He was paying absolutely no attention to me, and neither was anybody else. I respected his talent, his fame, but suddenly I thought, this could go on until three o'clock in the morning. If I just sneak out quietly nobody will know I'm gone. So I went home to Brooklyn. George called me the next morning and said, "What happened to you?" I replied, "I didn't think you knew I was there. After all, if I'm just going to sit and listen to you play all night, I can buy a record." He laughed and said, "Okay. I got carried away. Next time you go to a party with me, you sit right on the bench." I said, "That will be better." George remained my good friend until I left for Hollywood in 1932. The last time I saw him was six months before he died, in 1938, at the age of 38.

CHAPTER NINE

My First Love

MY MOTHER was still disturbed because I spent so little time at home; and she couldn't understand my complete absorption in my career or lack of interest in boys. I was in love with my career and in love with love, and adamant about my standards.

I rarely brought anybody home, because Mother would ask the boy too many personal questions, and she always sounded too eager to push me into marriage. I couldn't do anything with her, so I gave up trying to make her change.

My father was different. He was very proud of me, and when I came to his office to see him I always found a write-up about me tacked up on the walls. His confidence and his approval gave me determination and strength. My mother, as I have already indicated, disapproved of my highfalutin ideas. My radio show, on which I sang and read poetry for fifteen minutes in the late morning, continued, and as I look back, I wonder if Mother resented it because *she* was the singer in the family. She never paid me a compliment.

Irving Hoffman was a close friend of Sidney Skolsky, the dynamic little newspaper columnist who succeeded Walter Winchell when Walter moved from one paper to another. All the newspaper men were nice to me. Sidney's eyes always twinkled whenever he said hello. I don't know that any of them were terribly impressed with me, and I didn't have a feeling that any of them felt I would fire the world, but they accepted me as part of the gang and always treated me with an attitude of "She's a good kid; let's give her a break when we can."

The press agents were another breed. I never got to know them well, but evidently I was good copy. When things got dull they could always draw on my escape from Russia and the beauty contest, and of course since I kept going in and out of pictures and plays, there was often a squib about my comings and goings. Every gag they could think of to get a mention for the show in question would be created to get my name in the paper, like walking up Broadway with an orchid corsage on my ankle. Some of the stunts were ridiculous but harmless and helped to keep my name alive. I was fortunate that I had chosen Barbara as my first name long before I dreamed that I would see it in print, and since "Barbara Barondess" was unusual and euphonious, it was not easily forgotten.

One afternoon while I was having coffee with S. N. Behrman and Ken Nicholson, I lamented that I had no play and no part in the offing. Ken gave me a copy of *The Barker* and told me to learn the leading part, being played by Claudette Colbert. He suggested he might be able to get me the job of understudy. Barrie gave me a copy of his *Second Man* and wrote on the flyleaf, "For Barbara—up in the clouds."

Then they thought of another possibility. They had been talking about a producer whom they both disliked immensely. He was the sensational current hope of the theater. Young, he had three hits running on Broadway, with about seven companies of each play all over the world. He had a magic touch. Jed Harris was one of the most controversial, talented, and dynamic producers ever to hit Broadway. His personality and his idiosyncrasies had become legend. He was an egomaniac; he had hypnotic charm, talent, and intelligence, and was a dropout from Yale, but nobody liked him. People were always talking about his antics and jokes. Anything screwy or shocking done by anyone in those days was attributed to him. It was said that George S. Kaufman once went to his apartment for a conference, and Jed opened the door stark naked. I had not yet met the man. I had heard that he was not easy to get an interview with, and I never had the courage to try to see him.

Barrie and Ken were discussing a play that he was casting and decided to get me an appointment with him. Barrie called, and, much to my surprise and excitement, made an appointment for me to see Harris that same afternoon. They both assured me that I would be able to handle this genius. Of course I had heard so many stories that I was prepared to dislike him instantly.

I walked into an ordinary office in the Sardi building on 44th Street. The office had a secretary at the front desk and a small switchboard. I had to wait at least twenty minutes, during which time I had a chance to go over and over what I was going to say. The secretary motioned for me to come with her, escorting me into a large office with an enormous desk. I was startled to see a slight, unshaven, homely man slouching in his chair and grinning in the most disarming way as he said, "Hello. What can I do for you?" He had enormous black pools for eyes that just bored through me. I never said one word of what I planned.

I felt as if electric shock had erased everything in my mind. He motioned me to sit down, and gently asked me again what he could do for me. In a kind of vapid way, I said, "You could give me a job in your new play." He said he was sorry but there was no part in it for me. The girl parts had been cast—but what was I doing for dinner?

In an absolute daze, I said, "Nothing." I completely forgot that I had promised Barrrie and Ken to have dinner with them and let them know about my interview. This was an entirely new experience. This man didn't resemble anybody I had ever met, and he caught me unaware. His manner was so gentle that he had to drag information out of me about my family and my background. Articulate me, always ready to roll off all the important experiences of her life and her credits in the theater, was speechless.

He took me to dinner. I don't remember where or what we ate. All I know is that all my resolutions and plans went out of the window that night. I fell madly in love. We ate and drank, and walked and talked. He was wonderful to listen to, so bright and knowledgeable about Russian classics. The hours flew like magic. Everything that happened that night was inevitable. The magnet of attraction was in full force. I didn't resist or mention that this was the first time. And he made no reference to my virginity. It would be easy to blame it on the amount of liquor we consumed. Or my own more than usual imbibing just to keep up with him. But that's too easy.

I was in a hypnotic trance. For me what happened that night was the ultimate act of love; nothing else entered my mind as I lay next to him, and found him fast asleep beside me.

My eyes wandered around his room. It looked like a cyclone had hit it—books, clothes, bedding. I looked at the clock beside his bed and a bolt struck me. I had to get home. I slipped out of bed reluctantly, to dress and sneak out of the apartment without waking my love! He looked so vulnerable that a wave of tenderness engulfed me. So this is what everyone is doing and talking about. So this is the thing called love. Nothing would ever be the same for me.

It was a golden chariot, not the subway that took me home. I had met my Svengali. He was no Greek god, but I thought he was beautiful. My infatuation was complete. The stories about his selfishness and cruelty were all erased, dissolved, and out of mind. I was sure that all the tale tellers must have been jealous.

During the next days, I walked on eggshells, dreaming and waiting for *the* phone call. I suffered through every torch song ever written. Dorothy Parker's story about the telephone call was my theme. I identified with Edna St. Vincent Millay and every song and story of undying love. I knew he was conscious that I was alive, because he did finally call and we went out several times. I was ready for his invitations at the drop of a hat. My torch flamed brightly. Suddenly my ambitions were pushed into the background. I only wanted him to be madly in love with me. The Metropolitan Museum became my haven and waiting room. I called home from there almost every hour, in the hope there might be a message from him. Of course, most of the time there was no message.

This went on for a couple of months. I was sleepwalking, going through the motions, and trying not to show it. There was no one to talk to, no one to confide in. I had no idea how to handle him and I didn't know how to walk away from him. He told me he had been married while he was at college, but he didn't say whether the marriage had been dissolved, and I didn't dare ask. I was at his beck and call.

One night, when I had a date with him, I decided to phone to verify the time of our appointment. By one of those strange flukes of fate, the operator answering my call asked me to hold; he was busy on another wire. She must have left the key open and I was able to hear him speak to another woman. I heard him say, "Of course I'll meet you, darling. I have another appointment, but it isn't important." I recognized Ruth Gordon's voice.

I slowly put down the receiver and walked out of the telephone booth. I couldn't breathe. I felt as if somebody had taken my intestines and tied them into a knot. I don't remember what I did that night. I know I sat somewhere in a stupor. I was bewildered and hurt. The love and energy that I was willing to pour out to him, I was pouring into a bottomless pail.

The gossip about Jed's promiscuity, women, and peculiar behavior was suddenly oozing out of the woodwork. He was being credited with carrying on affairs with Ruth Gordon, Judith Anderson, Katharine Hepburn, Margaret Sullavan and heaven knows how many others. How he managed all this nobody could explain, except that everybody said that he was in bed more hours than he was out of it, around the clock. The more I heard the more ashamed I was to have fallen in love with him. It made me feel used and unclean. The shock and humiliation were so great that I determined to keep the whole unfortunate experience a secret for the rest of my life. To have fallen for his glib tongue and charms made me furious with myself. He was obviously a better actor than any he employed, with a brilliant brain, sardonic sense of humor and his particular brand of insecurity. He obviously wanted power to own and manipulate talent and beauty . . . the two things he really didn't believe he had. He became obsessed about being the mentor of all the young writers, directors, and actors who needed him, and he tried to control all of them, along with his harem. I don't believe that any woman in his life has ever gotten away from him completely, or ever forgotten him. He was a unique contradiction of brains, charm, talent, and behavior that bordered on insanity. When he was rational, he was irresistible.

Jed was instantly a part of me. I never heard anyone express himself with such passion and clarity about the theater as Jed. He had a hypnotic power that engulfed me. I felt as if he were taking my thoughts out of my head, and he made me aware of how empty my life was at home, and why I was so bored.

The years in Poland waiting for God's dispensation in the form of my American passport, and those stops and starts of hope and disappointment took their toll, more than we realized. We all ached in silence, and my father's voiceless voice with the ever present pencil and pad next to him used to tear my heart. It was now almost eight years since we left Russia, and almost ten years since Father lost his voice. The forced speech he developed was such a strain that after a few phrases uttered with great difficulty, he would resort to writing. And although we were in our dreamed-of America, I found Brooklyn depressing, along with our routines and lifestyle during that time, which only whetted my need and hunger for conversation and communication and the lifestyle of my childhood before the war and Revolution. So it was absolutely natural for me to long for the world beyond the Brooklyn Bridge. The art, theater, music, glimpses of the social life, was the magic string that led me to Broadway. It took a long time for me to understand what attracted me to Jed, and I still wonder how I had the strength to walk away from him. The only way I can explain it is that my hurt was so deep, and my pride so strong, that I refused to settle for being part of a harem. And that's what helped keep my affair with Jed my best kept secret for over fifty years. I would never give him the satisfaction of knowing how I felt, or mention it until after his death.

And as the old expression, "Time heals everything," comes to my mind, I go through the list of the interesting and talented women who also fell for him. I have the consolation at least that I was in very good company. The only three times that I saw him in the next thirty years were fascinating in retrospect, because the attraction became dimmer and dimmer each time. The last time I saw the man who wrecked himself with his own madness, I felt tremendous pity for the waste of a unique talent. As a producer and director who revolutionized Broadway as it became known after his first hit, *Broadway*, his was at one and the same time, the most promising and brilliant yet most destructive and erratic talent to hit twentieth century New York theater. His split personality and brilliance evoked love and hate to the point where the people whose lives he touched ended up hating him, except for a very few like Jean Dalrymple, who remained a friend to the end. All I know, in my own analysis of my reactions, was that I was afraid of him and his lack of control, exaggerated rebellion, quick tongued cruelty, and treatment of fragile creative talents. He seemed on the edge of insanity. Many outlived him and went on to make great careers for themselves, although he was ruthless to them. He died an unfortunate cruel death, penniless, alone, forgotten and mostly disliked.

My experience was more painful than anything I have ever felt, and it took me a long time to get over that hurt. Never again was I able to commit myself so completely to a man.

That first encounter with physical love made it impossible for me to be completely subjective in a relationship with a man for the rest of my life. I felt affection and attraction, but never again would I lose myself completely. The shock of the rejection taught me not to expect, ever, another person to make me happy.

Probably one of my burning inspirations from then on was not only to become a good actress but to become something special, somebody useful. I was, however, still determined that I would be married once someday. I was looking for an impossible combination of Prince Charming and my father.

When I pulled myself together, I started to call on producers' offices again. My "love" called me a couple of times. He had no way of knowing that I had heard his telephone conversation. He never discussed the night we had the date, because he had called my house and left a message that he couldn't keep the appointment. He reacted rather strangely when I made excuses for not seeing him, but I couldn't face him. I was afraid I'd break down.

After three or four more calls I agreed to meet him for dinner. I was frustrated with the desire to see him and the fear that I would make a fool of myself. I prayed for God to give me the right words and the composure to behave the way I should. The evening I was to see Jed again, I went to see Al Woods earlier in the day. He was the first producer I had ever met. His secretary told him I was outside and he asked me to come into his office. There were three people sitting there. He introduced me and said that they were casting the British company of a great hit then, 1927, running on Broadway with Ann Harding and Rex Cherryman—*Trial of Mary Dugan.* Tallulah Bankhead was slated to play the Ann Harding role in London. Did I want to play a part there? If I did, I'd have to leave that evening. I was flabbergasted but asked, "What about a passport?" He said, "Don't worry about the passport or money. We'll take care of everything. The boat sails at eight p.m. It's the maiden voyage return trip of the *Ile de France.* All you have to do is get your clothes and your trunk from Brooklyn."

So God came to my rescue again. I called my parents and persuaded my mother to pack everything she could of my best things. Mr. Woods said his office would cut the red tape and someone from downtown would come up with the passport. I called my undying love to tell him I was leaving and couldn't keep our date. I hoped that he would say, "Don't go. I'll miss you," but his words were, "Isn't that nice? Have a good trip."

I had four hours to sailing time. I took the subway to Brooklyn. Mother was numb, Father philosophical. He said, "Stella, our princess is twenty years old. We don't have to worry about her. If she can't take care of herself now, she never will." He put his arm around me and said, "If this is what you want and it's that important to you, go and God bless you."

Nineteen twenty seven. First class on the luxury liner *Ile de France*, six years after the ride on the *Celtic* in steerage. First class passengers included Archie Selwyn, Broadway producer; Ray Goetz, Broadway producer married to Irene Bordoni; Barbara Hutton, eighteen-year-old beautiful, fat rich girl; David Mdivani, the youngest of the Georgian penniless princes, looking for an heiress; the great French writer, André Maurois; the great French war hero and flying ace, René Funk; and many more, all rich and famous, and me. I couldn't help chuckling when the purser put me at the captain's table. At least I could get a laugh out of it. All this because I went swimming in Steeplechase Park and one thing led to another. This should have been a glorious trip for me, but it wasn't. I was devastated and heartbroken, although I was given star treatment.

Before the boat reached our destination, I had a wire from the Woods office telling me there was some difficulty with Miss Bankhead; rehearsals were postponed for two weeks. If I wanted to go to Paris, I could; money would be waiting for me with instructions at American Express.

In Paris I met an attractive young couple, Mr. and Mrs. John Jacobson, on their honeymoon. He was with the publishing house of Simon and Schuster. They took me under their wing and showed me everything in the city. They took me to a place on the Rue Blondel that turned out to be a whorehouse—a famous one, I later learned—where we were supposed to watch an *exhibition* by a few of *les girls*. When they brought out the props, I was so startled that I shut my eyes and kept them closed through the whole performance. The Jacobsons didn't notice that their shocked guest wasn't watching the show.

I met a French producer and owner of a nightclub in Paris, called "La Florida," who had heard me on the boat during "Gala Night," when I was asked to perform at the suggestion of Archie Selwyn. He offered me a job singing in the nightclub for a few weeks. I told him I would let him know; it depended on the rehearsals.

They never did patch up the differences with Tallulah Bankhead. The play never went on. I accepted the job in La Florida and sang there two weeks with an American orchestra. All the Americans who came to the night club introduced themselves to me sooner or later and Monta Bell, a Hollywood director of note, came almost every night and offered to give me a movie test at Paramount when I got back to New York. I also met a nice young Frenchman by the name of Robert Boris, who was with the Paramount French office, and serving his stint in the army. He was stationed at Fontainebleau. One afternoon I took a taxi to visit him there, not realizing that it was many miles away. The fare practically wiped me out for the week.

I spent the days going to the Louvre, drinking in the beauty of Paris.

I suppose I sang my torch ballads with a great deal of sincerity. I identified with every heartbroken wail. I think I almost enjoyed being sorry for myself. I was a full grown, heartbroken, disillusioned young woman. Everybody was on the make. Maurois, with his broken English, Selwyn, Goetz, anybody you could think of. The more they tried to win me over, the less responsive I became. I wasn't going to make another mistake.

I decided to go home. I sailed for New York on the *Paris* and was greeted on arrival like a visiting princess. If it weren't so funny, I wouldn't have kept the newspaper.

There was a possibility for me to replace a soubrette part in a play by Avery Hopwood. Hopwood was credited with coining the expression "gold diggers" when he wrote a play by that title.

He was a prolific writer, successful, but an incurable alcoholic. I believe the play, *The Garden of Eden*, was his last. One night in Nice, in 1928, while very drunk, he walked into the surf and drowned.

Miriam Hopkins was starring in this with Robert Montgomery, and Edward Knopf directing. The play had opened for a tryout in Boston, and was now moved to Washington. It was scheduled to open on Broadway two weeks later. I was to get there as fast as I could, to play the second lead. I didn't think Miriam Hopkins would remember me, but I remembered her. A week before I left for Paris, I was having lunch with Horace Liveright and Theodore Dreiser. She was rehearsing for *An American Tragedy*. When she spotted us at the table, she came right over and started to gush. I don't think she stopped for five minutes. The men never opened their mouths, and she ignored me completely. Her date pulled her away, and, as she left, Horace rolled his eyes and said, "Nobody could be as enthusiastic about anything as she is about everything."

Getting the part in *The Garden of Eden* came at the perfect time for my broken heart and injured ego. When I got home from Paris, Father and Mother couldn't hear enough about my trip, First Class, in a cabin all to myself on the maiden voyage of a luxury ship like the *Ile de France*. I had to tell them about the cabin, the entertainment, the food, the people, what they wore and what they said. Father's eyes shone as he said, "I always knew that my princess would some day travel in style." To this, Mother added an expression that I can remember her uttering most of her life, "From your mouth to God's ears." My father said, "I know, my darling, that you will not let all this publicity and attention go to your head. I know you are intelligent enough to realize that exterior beauty is a gift from God. You had nothing to do with it, and it's not given forever. It's a gift to youth and only a preparation to what you do with it and how much influence it will have on your life."

So much had happened to me since I won that contest. Before I left for Paris, I had been asked to appear on the Judges' Panel for the new Miss Greater New York. The result was more publicity to keep my name in print. Added to the two plays I had already appeared in on Broadway, it didn't hurt my status.

I had met many super rich young men as a result of my trip to Europe and as my social activities broadened. Billy Seeman, heir to the White Rose canned fruit fortune, invited me to dinner at Mayor Jimmy Walker's house. The mayor was handsome and debonair, well known in theater circles, and the night I met him was romancing Phyllis Haver, a then current silent movie star, whom he eventually married.

Going home to Brooklyn on the subway made me feel like Cinderella at midnight, and no matter how wealthy my dates were, I discouraged their taking me home by taxi, and insisted they escort me to the subway station, but I had to go home alone. The subways were safe and usually deserted, but I preferred that to fighting off my dates in an hour ride in the back of a taxi cab. I was dying for an apartment of my own in New York, but I just couldn't hurt my father and I knew that my mother would be hysterical. So, I had to bide my time until I could talk to him about it. Father listened carefully to everyone. He never lost his temper, not even way back in my early youth, with my mother's temper and screaming and quick apologies two minutes later. I wonder if it's so natural for me or the example of my father that has made it difficult ever to lose my temper. I'm a very slow burner. It takes me a long time to be disappointed in someone. But once I am, I am finished forever.

The soubrette part in *The Garden of Eden* was set. I was to join the play in Washington. The tickets and instructions with the script of my part were delivered to me. This was the first part I had been offered that I didn't know anything about. The producers had asked for me, and I knew only that I was replacing another actress.

The first few days I was home, I didn't feel quite normal. On waking, the nausea was disturbing and new. I was afraid to let the family know. Lenore Wilder, my close friend since *Gay Paree*, was the only one I confided in about my devastating romance with Jed. Her reaction was shock, and that led me to a doctor, who corroborated her suspicion and my fear.

I was almost three months pregnant, had to report for the play in four days, and had gained six pounds.

The thought of having this love child was paralyzing. My parents would be heartbroken if they learned about it, and I would be disgraced. How could I bring an illegitimate child into the world and support it? It was out of the question. The only answer, abortion, was demoralizing and frightening.

The doctor warned me that I didn't have any time to lose. My life was at stake, as he gave me the name of the only abortionist he said would do it that same evening.

My head was whirling. "Pray for guidance; make the best of everything," Father had said so often. I had no choice. This was my mistake. I had handed myself to Jed on a platter, and he had helped himself. I couldn't honestly blame him, and my independence would not allow me to let him know or ask for help.

Fortunately I had the $300 in cash needed for the abortionist in the Bronx, and enough to cover a hotel room for a couple of days before going to Washington.

Lenore came home with me for moral support. I was so afraid I would give myself away, and I prayed that I would not see my father. Fortunately, he was staying at his office late. I packed in a frenzy, and Lenore and I went back to New York to check into the Piccadilly Hotel on 45th Street.

I asked Lenore to please wait for me in the hotel. I felt that I had to go to the Bronx alone. She was a beautiful but high-strung girl, and a worrier. I was cool and objective, as I was to be most of my life, in the face of tragedy and disappointment. I had to be alone on this sad taxi ride to the Bronx, to sort out my priorities.

It was a lonely trip. I felt terribly sad that I was on my way to kill my first child, of my first love. I was desperately in love, and knew that he didn't love me.

The taxi pulled up in front of a dark brown wooden private dwelling. My appointment was for eight p.m. It was 7:45 when I paid the taxi and rang the bell.

A nondescript woman in a nurse's uniform opened the door, asked my name, took the $300 and told me to sit down. After she disappeared through the door, my eyes grew accustomed to the barely lit room. At my side sat a woman with a young girl who looked as if she had been crying, not more than fourteen years old. Across the room was a young couple, the woman in her twenties with a thin young man about the same age. He had a protective arm around her and her face turned away from me as soon as she saw me look her way.

I looked at the other ignorant fools who didn't know enough to protect themselves.

The nurse appeared again and took the fourteen-year-old with her. The older woman wanted to go too, but the nurse insisted that she wait outside. She sat down, an apprehensive expression on her face. I wondered what the operation was like, when I heard an agonizing scream. We all jumped, and in unison clutched our mouths. The young woman started to cry. I was paralyzed with fear. The next five minutes were an eternity. The nurse opened the door a crack and motioned the mother to come in. Then she opened the door again and motioned to me. I entered another room with brighter light, an office and operating room combination. The desk had two chairs, one on each side. The operating table was to one side, covered with a rubber sheet, over which the nurse was putting a linen sheet, while the doctor asked a couple of questions. He was a big man with a big head and big hands. He looked more like a butcher than a doctor. I was asked to raise my dress and take off my panties, and was placed on the table with my legs in stirrups, the second time in one day in the humiliating position that every woman is subjected to for a gynecological examination. The doctor thrust a metal object into me and proceeded to scrape and probe. I bit my lip at this brutal, painful act, administered without sedative or pain killer.

In about seven minutes he was packing me with cotton. My whole body hurt, and the muscles in my stomach were in excruciating pain from trying to hold my breath. The whole business took about fifteen minutes. I wanted just to lie on the table to catch my breath.

But the nurse put her arm under my shoulders to sit me up. I begged the nurse to let me rest a few minutes, but she said no, sorry, the young lady outside was next. There was a taxi outside waiting to take me home. She opened the back door, a taxi driver helped me into the cab, and I stretched out in the back seat, with my head and body flat and my knees doubled up holding them with my arms to relieve the pain. I felt sick to my stomach. It was over. I had killed my baby. I had to do it, for my parents, for my future. I prayed never to make this same mistake again.

Lenore was waiting in the lobby. She squeezed my hand as she led me to the elevator. I got into bed immediately, and after she ordered some hot bouillon for me, I fell into a dead sleep. I was to pay for that abortion for the rest of my life.

Youth, good health and the will to get well got me through the next three days. I made the train to Washington on schedule. I was surprised to find the director of the play, Edwin Knopf, on it. While we were talking in the club car, Douglass Montgomery walked in. I was surprised to see him, and more surprised when I learned that he was to replace Robert Montgomery. This was a happy reunion for me, and I felt a curious release from apprehension.

Douglass and I had become friends during the rehearsals and run of *Crime.* We had had a few dates while the show was on the road, and after it opened in New York, and established a camaraderie that was relaxed and easy. I admired his confidence and poise and no-nonsense dedication to his responsibility as an actor. Although he was young, about twenty, he behaved like a seasoned pro and commanded respect. He was six feet tall, handsome in a clean-cut American way. There was nothing sloppy about him.

The train arrived early in the morning and we checked into

the Ritz Hotel. Rehearsals were called for about two hours later. There wasn't much time and I rushed to unpack the little I had and take a bath, because I was anxious to get a glimpse of the capital of my country. I was told the theater was a few blocks away, a short walk. When I had gone a block and was walking past a long iron fence, I realized that I was looking at the White House. As I turned a corner, my eyes were still on the White House. Suddenly I felt a bump and both of my arms were grabbed and pinned back; I looked into the astonished face of the President of the United States, Calvin Coolidge.

Two men were holding my arms. I was crimson, hot, and speechless. I didn't know how to address him. I started to say, "Mister," and a whole speech poured out: "Excuse me, President, forgive me. I'm terribly sorry. I didn't mean to knock you off your feet. I never dreamed of seeing you in person. It's my first time in Washington and I never dreamed when we got out of Russia that I would get this close to the White House or the President of the United States, my country, where I was born on the same day you were born, the Fourth of July."

His face lit up. He gave me a warm smile and motioned to the two plainclothesmen to let me go. In my excitement, I kept on, "I apologize, I'm sorry, but in a way I'm glad because I would never have met you if I hadn't been struck so dumb by the excitement of being here." I literally backed away as I waved goodbye, and ran across the street against traffic. When I got across, I saw the President waving goodbye, the unsmiling President of the United States with a big grin on his face.

When I walked into the theater it took a few seconds for my eyes to get used to the darkness. There were several people in the dim light sitting about half way down in the middle of the theater. A single work light glowed on the stage, and a couple of prop men were setting out some chairs for the rehearsal. I walked down the aisle to see who was sitting in the middle rows and slid into the empty chair next to Douglass Montgomery. I was bursting to share my experience and started to tell it to Douglass without realizing that my stage whisper could be heard by everybody in the row. He introduced me to the two men on his right. My eyes had accustomed themselves to the light, so I could see the round-faced man sitting next to Douglass, whose name I didn't catch. And the distinguished gentleman next to him, Douglass whispered, was Mr. Taylor, the manager of the theater. They were amused by my story. Suddenly I heard my name called for the run-through on stage. When the rehearsal was over I received a message that Mr. Taylor wanted me to see him in his office.

Mr. Taylor asked if I would like to visit the White House. All I could say to that was, "You must be kidding." He said, "No, Douglass Montgomery told me about your fascinating background, and the gentleman who was sitting next to me can arrange it. He thought that the President might enjoy seeing you again." I thought, How ridiculous! I can go to the White House because I almost knocked the President off his feet, and by a strange coincidence I was born on his birthday. Suddenly my birthdate had added importance for me.

Mr. Taylor wrote the following letter to the gentleman I had met in the theater whose name I hadn't recognized:

September 24, 1927

My dear friend Hoover:

Will you if nothing prevents today kindly let Miss Barondess of our company have a look over the White House. Miss Barondess is playing her first engagement in Washington and would much appreciate the courtesy.

Kindest regards.
Sincerely yours,

L. S. Taylor

I flew out of his office down the street, clutching the precious letter. It was noon and I didn't have to be at rehearsals in the afternoon because Douglass' part was being rehearsed and we never appeared on stage at the same time. (I had practically learned my whole part the night before, on the train, and we were to step into our roles two days later.) I presented my letter at the South Gate of the White House and at the door, walked into an exquisite foyer with the reception room to the right, and joined a line that was passing the President, who stood with Herbert Hoover on his right and the same plainclothesmen who grabbed my arms early in the morning. As the procession passed in front of the President, he pressed each visitor's hand and spoke a couple of words. When his eyes met mine, his face lit up with a grin, and he said, "Nice to see you again." Hoover was next to shake my hand. As he did, he whispered, "Step aside and wait right here behind me." I stepped out of line and stood behind Hoover for about five minutes until the line ended. There I was, standing about three feet away from the President and thinking, "Isn't this heaven! I'm actually going to see the White House." Hoover gave me back the letter to keep as a souvenir and told me that the President had invited me to lunch. Then they would both show me the White House.

I sat at the oblong table next to Secretary Hoover. I believe there must have been ten to twelve people, most of them men. I don't remember the food. All I could think of was the magic of fate. I looked at the smiling, friendly face of Coolidge, whose reputation for being so poker faced seemed to me unwarranted as I noted the amusement in his eyes whenever he glanced my way. After lunch, as Hoover and I walked out of the dining room, the President joined us and said to me, "The thing you said yesterday about being in Russia and being born in the United States intrigued me. How did you happen to be in Russia?" And there I was telling Coolidge and Hoover my story. I was so used to telling it that I rattled it off while I looked at the pictures and drank in the sights of the furniture and rooms we walked through. Coolidge asked if I knew Al Jolson. I told him I did, and he said, "I like him very much. A great performer, and also born on our birthday." So I learned that Jolson was a Fourth of July baby, and was also able to give him the President's regards the next time I saw him. Coolidge apologized for the fact that the White House furniture still had its slipcovers on. He said that Mrs. Coolidge was out of town and as soon as she returned at the end of the week they would be removed. It was the first time I had ever heard of "slipcover."

CHAPTER TEN

Hollywood—Ten Times Larger Than Life

THE GARDEN OF EDEN lasted only twenty performances—it closed in March 1928—but it was time enough for my friendship with Douglass Montgomery to grow strong enough to last a lifetime. It was a unique bond—with affection, tenderness, and no strings—between two people who enjoyed each other's company and could talk about anything together, do whatever they felt like doing without inhibition, and completely get rid of their frustrations. We liked each other, without falling in love. It was fun; it was beautiful. We filled each other's needs without promises. We never explained, complained or analyzed. We both knew that we had something unique and precious without discussing it.

After *The Garden of Eden* closed, Douglass went into *Volpone* with Alfred Lunt and Lynn Fontanne. I met and saw quite a bit of a young English actor playing his first part in *Journey's End,* an English hit by R.C. Sherriff. His name was Jack Hawkins. He was a thin, shy young man who played the coward. We had a casual but pleasant time together while the play was running, and I got to know the English cast.

I lost track of Jack when he went back to England. He later married Jessica Tandy. When he matured he became a big star, and whenever I saw that virile, square-jawed, poised man on the screen I recalled the skinny, gawky, shy kid with adolescent acne who played in *Journey's End*. (It was more than thirty years later that I read he had cancer of the throat. I wrote to him in England, and saw him again in Palm Beach in 1972, when he came to make a personal appearance in connection with the film, *Young Winston*, in which he played a voiceless part. Jack died not long afterward, in 1973.)

Although I was jobless in the theater, I wasn't too discouraged. I no longer had to rely on the title of Miss Greater New York but was accepted as a member of the acting profession and a regular at Sardi's. I went back to my fifteen minutes on radio, now five times a week, which I could leave and return to any time. Some of my dates would take me to Jack and Charlie's, which became Jack Kriendler and Charlie Burns' "21," or to the exclusive a backgammon speakeasy owned by John Perona and Jim Moriarty. Perona was to open the El Morocco after Prohibition, while Jim Moriarty became the host of the Barberry Room. Jim was a backgammon champion who taught me how to play the game. I occasionally went to dinner at his apartment, and his cook taught me some of her marvelous Southern recipes.

The other friends, some who could barely afford a cup of coffee, were young and ambitious actors, writers, directors like Chester Erskine and composers like George Gershwin; and of course the Three Musketeers—Irving Hoffman, Marcel Morel and Harry Sternberg. The drawing lessons they gave me helped me to appreciate art even more. The Metropolitan Museum was still my haven. It was easy to get to for a nickel on the bus, and I spent many afternoons there between appointments.

The acting jobs were erratic. I was given the soubrette role in a musical called *Rain or Shine*, starring Joe Cook, with Dave

Chasen, who later started the renowned Beverly Hills restaurant that bears his name. He was Cook's "stooge." The soubrette was a character called Frankie, who had a couple of songs to sing and did a little dancing. Her big number was a song "Add a Little Wiggle," performed in a hula costume. The producers couldn't make up their minds on the type that should play this part. They broke all records by having twenty Frankies before it opened on Broadway. I think I was number fourteen, and I got to play it in Buffalo. But even before each girl opened, they had already hired another one who stood by to step into the part one week later. That's the only time I've ever been fired in the theater.

I avoided romantic involvement—I suppose as much because I'd been rejected as because no one answered my requirements. Although my opportunities seemed varied and rich, nobody appealed to me. Douglass Montgomery was fun, but something was missing. I was not a Prohibition liquor-guzzling flapper. I learned how to spill drinks into flower pots in order not to look like a square, and I always apologized to God for hurting the plants.

That was the era of the "Vitaphone" talking pictures frenzy. Every studio had talent scouts in New York who set up endless tests on every promising actor and actress. Monta Bell made good his promise to give me a screen test with sound, and I was fortunate enough to have Eddy Duchin accompanying me as I sang a couple of songs. I had met Eddy while dancing at the Casino in the Park (Central Park), where he was the star attraction with Leo Reisman's orchestra. But nothing came of the test.

The first movie tests were made by newsreel cameramen who were used to photographing sailings of the *Leviathan* and football games and such. They knew nothing about highlighting facial features to bring out your best qualities. Even if you looked as good as Garbo, the screen test could make you look like hell. I wasn't lucky. Some of my contemporaries, however, were getting Hollywood contracts. Sylvia Sidney was on her way. So were Kay Francis, Ginger Rogers, Barbara Stanwyck, and

Miriam Hopkins. They were the first crop of Broadway actresses to make it to movie heaven and were getting the star build-up treatment.

With the new talkies, the silent screen stars were dropping from sight, dying from drugs and liquor. They couldn't cope with success and were copping out with failure. The suicides were horrendous—Barbara LaMarr, Alma Rubens, Olive Thomas, Wallace Reid. Broadway was producing a new crop of stars—Muriel Kirkland, Katharine Hepburn—and supporting a few great ones who were not photogenic—Katharine Cornell, the Lunts, Jane Cowl, Phoebe Foster, Eugenie Leontovich.

The MGM scout in New York was Al Altman, a short man, quiet, with a sensitive face. I had dinner with him once and he asked me if I would make a test. I got to know his loyal secretary, Marian Landsman. She liked me and whenever she heard of anybody making tests of New York actresses, she suggested me. But nothing happened. Finally, I got the message and decided I just wasn't motion picture material. To begin with, most movie actresses were between five feet and five feet three inches, and weighed about a hundred pounds. They were mostly flat-chested, delicate, small girls that today we call size four or six. I was 5'4", 118 pounds—healthy and wholesome girl with a full feminine figure. My type just wasn't in style. I was disappointed, but I told myself that one cannot have everything, and I concentrated on perfecting my craft as a stage actress.

I still hated our dingy house in Brooklyn. I mentioned to Marcel Morel one day how drab the muddy pink walls of my bedroom were, and he offered to help me paint them. One afternoon I called Mother and asked her to please have dinner ready for us. Marcel and I arrived there with a can of skyblue paint and a bag of dry silver powder. Marcel said the powder was for a surprise.

By midnight, we finished painting the room blue, then came the surprise. Marcel made a cone out of paper, put the silver powder into it, and blew at one end so the powder stuck to the wet paint in the form of a silver snowflake. The result was spectacular. By two a.m., Mother was hysterical. Father thought it the funniest sight he'd ever seen. The walls were beautiful, pale blue with silver stars, and Marcel and I had silver paint in our hair, eyebrows, eyelashes and clothes. My mother couldn't understand a word of what Marcel was saying, because his French accent was so thick. I'm sure she thought we both were absolutely out of our minds. Rosalie and Lucy had a ball.

On Saturdays and Sundays I would go horseback riding in Prospect Park. I was afraid of horses, but Father had bought me beautiful, expensive riding boots and jodhpurs, and I didn't dare disappoint him. One day as I was riding along, I met a tall, good looking, shy, hazel-eyed young man who said he was working at his first job, on Wall Street. He was such a contrast from my other friends that I enjoyed riding with him. We saw each other quite a few times. I never let him come home with me, though, because I was afraid Mother would pounce on him. He looked like such a good possibility for the future husband she envisioned for me. His name was Irving Jacobs.

One day in August, the paths were muddy after a heavy rain, our horses were walking side by side, and I was dangling my feet out of the stirrups. My horse tripped and threw me against a tree. I was knocked unconscious. Irving brought me home and my parents called the doctor. I had to to stay in bed for six weeks with a fractured vertebra. Irving was sweet and attentive. He came to see me often, and he fell in love.

It was nice to have someone adore me for a change, and when he asked me to marry him, I saw no point in saying that I didn't really love him. Although I was fond of Irving, at that time I didn't believe I could ever love anybody. Jed was still in my bones. The temptation was great, however, and my desire to get out of the house was strong. This seemed the perfect solution.

I told him I would think about it. He told me he was doing well in Wall Street, that early fall of 1929. I wondered how honest it was for me to marry him without telling him about my disastrous love affair. I decided not to. If I married I would be a good wife and raise a family. But he didn't object to my career in the theater—in fact he was fascinated with it—so I could go on acting.

The day after I agreed to marry him, the stock market collapsed. I had no idea of the devastation and importance of the crash until I realized that people were jumping out of windows, and, it seemed, everybody was going broke. The day after the crash, we went to Borough Hall in Brooklyn and were married.

Irving and I told no one about it. After the "ceremony" in a dingy registrar's office, we came to my house to announce it to my parents. Mother was hysterical. Father was silent. I felt guilty about not having told him. When Mother calmed down, Father said, "It's done. Let's take it from here. I've been saving some money in the hope that my oldest daughter would marry a nice young man one day, and I would have joy and pleasure in giving her away. The wedding is over but the money is there. What would you like to do with it?"

I was stunned and more ashamed to have robbed him of the pleasure, but I was my father's daughter and practical, so I said we could use the money to furnish our apartment. He said that would be fine.

No jet could carry me faster than the subway to New York the next morning to look for an apartment. I had been in a building at One West 67th Street, at Central Park West, called Des Artistes. I was pleased to find that they had a duplex studio apartment. It consisted of a large, bilevel living room, one small bedroom upstairs, and a tiny kitchen on the first floor with a dumbwaiter that led to a basement restaurant where you could order food sent up. The rent was, I suppose, high for that time, considering the crash. It was a little under $300 a month. But it would have been perfect—if Irving had not lost his job that day.

With my usual optimism I figured out that we could afford it since I averaged around $250 a week with all my odd jobs and of course there was the hope that Irving would find work. I took the apartment on a three-year lease. With the money that Father gave me I bought a beautiful grand piano. A piano and a bed were two basic pieces of furniture in my life, although I never learned to play.

My first Christmas in my own home . . . just eight years removed from Ellis Island . . . I couldn't believe it. My blessed, generous, kind father, who worked so hard and never complained, had made it possible. It was the American Dream just beginning. My heart was filled with so much gratitude that it pushed out any guilt I still had about Jed and about not really being in love with Irving. But I had made up my mind that he would never know. I was convinced that I could never fall in love again. The apartment was smashing, with a bare minimum to start. Even if we had had the money, I wanted to do it slowly. A Louis XV desk, a simple sofa and a couple of chairs done in beige velvet, one enormous green bottle made into a lamp for the piano, a bed, and a couple of chests and mirrors, a folding bridge table and four chairs for dining—and that was the end of our capital. Only one lamp, and one drawing of Otto Kahn. The bilevel living room looked bare but stunning. Finally I had something tasteful to live with.

A few days after we moved in, we went to Irving's family in Brooklyn for our first Sunday meal. He had two older sisters, one married, the other not. I found out quickly that his mother was terribly disappointed in his marriage. She couldn't care less if I were Miss America, and the fact that I was an actress didn't impress her. She kept saying how lucky I was that the apple of her eye had married me without a dowry. She told me of opportunities he had had to marry Jewish princesses with wealthy fathers. It was no use pointing out to her that my father was worth a million rich fathers. I didn't even point out that her prize was out of a job and I was the breadwinner.

I was ecstatic with our new home. Now I saw Brooklyn only once a week, when we visited Irving's parents. My own family I invited to dinner with us in Manhattan, and that gave me a chance to practice my cooking. Irving started looking for work but never found any.

One day in January 1930 I got a call from the Shubert office. I went to see Lee Shubert, and he told me they had a French play by Marcel Pagnol called *Topaze* that was opening at the Music Box in two days, January 30. The ingenue lead had just informed him she was pregnant. He was furious, and asked me to replace her. It sounded wonderful; the only catch was my predecessor had to perform the role on opening night. My salary was to be $300 a week. I said thank you, grabbed the script, and went home to study. The play was enchanting. My part was that of an insipid ingenue—nothing to give a dramatic performance in, just a foil for Frank Morgan. There was one other woman in the play.

A showcase. Too bad I couldn't open in it and maybe get some critical attention, but I thought, it's a step up. *They* called *me*. The play had an important cast: Frank Morgan, Clarence Derwent, Harry Bannister, and Phoebe Foster, an elegant lady well known for leading roles in Philip Barry drawing-room comedies. The thought of walking across the same stage with them for $300 a week was exhilarating, a windfall.

Topaze was an instant hit. Frank Morgan's name went up in lights on the marquee for the first time as a star. Everybody in the cast was mentioned favorably. I stepped into the part on the second night. Lucky for me I was the darling of the media. Irving Hoffman drew a smashing caricature of me, and the newspapers announced my joining the cast as if I were an important replacement. The company was happy because the publicity I got meant more attention to the show, and I continued to be mentioned in newspapers and magazines for the run of the play. Sam Marks was the publicity man.

So at last I had a steady job *and* a husband. Now I had a chance to entertain my theatrical friends, and Irving got to meet them. The other Irving in my life, Hoffman, had become friendly with Helen Morgan, and he brought her over. I loved the apartment, and the future looked promising. That year, thanks to Irving Hoffman's newspaper connections, I was invited to write an occasional "gossip" column in the *Morning*

Telegraph. The paper's editor-in-chief was Whitney Bolton, a lovely man. When I brought my copy in and he handed it to the City Desk, the boys used to vie for the honor of correcting my spelling. The column would fill anywhere from six to ten inches, and I got two dollars an inch. I titled it "Little Bo-Peep on Broadway."

My good luck was sheltering me from the miseries of the Depression which, I only half realized, was devastating millions of people. Fortunately, Father's business held up. Mother became his star saleswoman, calling on people to get printing orders. He always gave her credit for getting the General Electric account.

The life of luxury chez Des Artistes, whose glamorous tenants included Fannie Hurst and Valentino's widow, Natasha Rambova, continued until late spring, when it dawned on me that we could not afford the rent much longer. No, not "we" but "I." Husband Irving still hadn't found a job. He went out regularly to look for one, or so he said, but times, as he kept reminding me, were bad. In addition, he said he couldn't take just *any* job—whatever he got had to match the kind of work and salary he had been getting in Wall Street before the crash. I told him that despite my *Topaze* salary and miscellaneous other bits of income, we would have to move. I couldn't carry the expenses alone. In his usual vague way, he shrugged, and let me do the apartment hunting.

It's true that I hadn't seen much of him, because in the mornings when he was "job-hunting," I cleaned the house and shopped for dinner, then sometimes had lunch at Sardi's in order to be seen, to keep in touch with my colleagues, and maybe to pick up a bit of news or information for my occasional *Morning Telegraph* column. Twice a week I had matinees, and, of course, six nights a week I had a performance. In addition, I was taking acting lessons from Clarence Derwent's sister, Alfreda, a well-known coach who specialized in Shakespeare. Ours became pretty much of a Sunday marriage.

Maybe I should have tried to imbue him with more ambition,

make demands that would force him to take any kind of a job to keep his self-respect. But I felt guilty and tried to make up for it by not making demands.

My writing the column gave me added status and the crude passes diminished. The country was entering a tumultuous decade in American history: the end of traditional values and idealism. Looming ahead were the ravages of the Great Depresssion and social welfare and reform. My marriage was empty, but I was too busy to give it much thought. And I felt that it was my own doing, and I had to make the best of it. This was the compromise I had made to get out of Brooklyn and be on my own. I didn't ignore Irving; I did everything a wife is supposed to do when I got the chance.

Meanwhile, I was paying the rent and tramping around in search of a less expensive place. When I found it—a railroad flat for $50 a month in a narrow building on West 63rd Street, next door to August Daly's Theater—I did the furnishing and decorating. I scrounged chairs and tables from friends. In Macy's basement I picked up a slightly damaged yellow sofa. I went to Dazian's, a famous source of theatrical fabrics, and got sixty yards of Indian handmade theatrical gauze, fringed with butterflies and insects, at thirty cents a yard, with which I made floor-length curtains to cover one entire wall that had windows looking west, over the roof of the theater where *White Cargo* was playing. There was plenty of light, fortunately. The floors, of light oak, had been stripped. There was a fireplace which I loved. The whole effect was surprisingly dramatic.

I got to know Irene Lee, who also lived in the building. She was a pianist who wanted to become an actress and was studying with Eva Le Gallienne. She became, instead, the youngest story editor at Warner Brothers and, in 1936, my first decorating client.

Having learned how to paint walls from Marcel Morel, I bought some paint, white and black, hoping my husband would get off his bottom and help me do the walls and furniture. But no, he didn't want to ruin his manicure or he always had an appointment. He would disappear; I was never sure where. I don't think he had many friends outside of those he met through me. I began to realize that he was a spoiled child—we were both only twenty-three. He was impressed with fame and money, but not sufficiently to work for either. I began to resent his caustic sense of humor, which was usually at other people's expense.

It was Barbara Barondess, not Mrs. Irving Jacobs, who did the work, and who was billed as "Ernestine Mouche" in the program for *Topaze* and cited in the newspaper columns by the Broadway reporters. So it happened that one night after the show, when Irving had picked me up at the theater because we had to go somewhere, as we were walking along I was surprised by an unexpected friend and started to make introductions. "This is my husband, Irving—Irving . . .," I stammered and let my voice fade. I couldn't remember his last name!

Our sex life was not very spectacular, because we were both really inexperienced. In those days, there were no descriptions depicting the *Joy of Sex* or manuals on the mechanics of love-making. At least not in my world. There were a lot of whispers and bottom-pinching, but unless one did considerable sleeping around, one didn't learn anything. I accepted Irving's catch-as-can lovemaking and it didn't excite me or bother me—because, I realize now, I was still too hurt and rigid to really let go and have fun.

Topaze ran through the summer. I went to see my family now and then, or they came into New York. I noticed that Father was growing thin, and that he was having more difficulty with his speech. He still, of course, loved to hear about my theatrical life, and he enjoyed reading about his Princess in the newspapers.

In October 1930, *Topaze* went on tour for almost five months. It was a valuable experience and a terrible trial. Our original company was intact except for the Phoebe Foster part, replaced by Katherine Willard, who was having a romance with Ralph Bellamy.

We began with a month in Chicago at the Princess Theatre.

Frank Morgan, of course, delighted the audiences, but we knew him as a heavy drinker who would go on stage smashed and try to break up the cast. He would do unexpected improvisations that could make an actor stumble over his lines or completely throw him. One night he did it to me, and I just couldn't continue. The stage manager brought the curtain down giving the audience some excuse about a problem backstage. We pulled ourselves together and the curtain went up again.

Morgan was threatened by Equity and he stopped doing his tricks for awhile. But he started them again and we were ready, but that wasn't good for the performances. I suppose he was bored with the part he had played for so long, and this was his way of showing it. Half the time on the road, when a play closed on Saturday night, somebody in the town would give a party for the cast. Morgan was always the last one at the party and usually so intoxicated that in the morning he couldn't get up to make the train for the next town. On three or four occasions Clarence Derwent and I were elected to stay over to make sure he got onto a train with us so we could make the performance on Monday night. It took us all day Sunday to sober him up. Usually we left his socialite wife Alma behind because she too was often indisposed. She would catch up with us by the middle of the week.

I had begun to learn about people with an alcohol problem when I got to know Horace Liveright. On this road trip I graduated. Frank Morgan was one and Helen Morgan, no relation, another. While we were playing in Chicago, Helen was also there in *Sweet Adeline* with Jimmy Dunn and Charles Butterworth. She invited me to stay in her big apartment with two bedrooms in the Sherman Hotel. During the month that I lived there I rarely saw her, and when I did it was usually at five in the afternoon, when the masseuse came to wake her up, give her a massage, sober her up with black coffee, and try to make her eat something light so she could get to the theater by seven, usually hastily bundled in a coat over a terry-cloth robe.

By the time the curtain went up no one would dream that she had been on a binge the night before and would start another one after the performance. I wondered what tormented her. She didn't last long enough for me to find out. She died in her early forties.

At the same time in Chicago there was another play called *The Last Mile*, with Spencer Tracy and John Beal. It was directed by Chester Erskine. Spencer had signed a contract for Hollywood and this was his last play. We celebrated with a going-away party before he left for the movies. There was also a Shubert musical with a fabulous Russian personality, Gregory Ratoff who was married to Eugenie Leontovich, and a young Englishman by the name of Archie Leach. Of course Archie Leach metamorphosed into the suave and fabulous Cary Grant. We all saw each other at the typical actors' parties and the regular hangouts. We rarely went to any good restaurants because we never had much money. Actors don't like to eat a heavy meal before a performance; it makes them too relaxed and logy. The usual routine is to wind down after a show, so we used to gather in the popular pubs frequented by actors; they all looked like one of our favorite places in New York, Billy LaHiff's Tavern.

In Chicago I remember the Bal Tabarin, which was very popular. Of course our escorts had to have the price. It had a fabulous organ on a suspended platform that was connected to a lighting device: light, color and form in constant motion. As the music played, it threw multicolored images on the wall which changed like a magnificent sunset as the organist, Thomas Wilfred, played his "Clavilux." It was a dreamy, enchanting "light show" to dance to and watch. We enjoyed going to parties at Ernie Byfield's and Frank Berring's—owners respectively of the Ambassador and Sherman hotels. They loved theater people and gave parties all the time, at which we got square meals. I met and went out with the attractive Chicago critic, Gale Borden.

After Chicago we took *Topaze* to several cities for one week each—Kansas City, Milwaukee, Minneapolis. (Oh, the bitter Wisconsin and Minnesota winters! I thought I would be frozen for the rest of my life.) Then Boston—the Plymouth Theatre for a month—and the Walnut Theatre in Philadelphia for another month. After the fun of Chicago, I stuck pretty much to myself. It was tiring: Christmas in Boston; New Year's in Philadelphia; Frank Morgan, a difficult alcoholic; my father growing weaker (as I learned from letters) . . . all in all, it was a bleak winter.

I had to send money to Irving to pay the rent, as well as gas and electricity and laundry and food bills, and I had my own hotel and food expenses on the road. Clarence Derwent taught me to salt away ten percent of my salary regularly. He had gotten the habit from Sir Henry Irving, who told him just to put away that amount and pretend that he was making ten percent less. Clarence, a fine character actor but never a star, seldom made more than $500 a week, but by the 1940's he had $100,000 in bonds. From these he derived the income he lived on, and was adding his salary to the principal. When he died, he left a sizeable fortune for the Clarence Derwent Foundation, which supports worthy actors and bestows the Clarence Derwent Award once a year on a promising actor or actress.

In the early spring of 1931, I came back from my first tour, exhausted, glad to be back in the electric atmosphere of New York City. But I was shocked when I went to Brooklyn to tell the family about my travels, to find Father even more pale and thin, almost transparent. To my horror I learned that he had terminal cancer of the throat. In those early days before the use of radioactive therapy, medical specialists knew even less about how to treat the disease than they do now. The treatments and the disease were wearing Father away.

Irving still had not found a job. I went back to my radio program, my news column, and occasional spots in night clubs. One day in June I went without any great expectations to Chamberlain Brown's office to see if there was anything open for me in a stock company. There were many such companies, of course, but the two most prominent were Jesse Bonestell's in Detroit and Robert McLaughlin's at the Hanna Theater in Cleveland. When I walked into the office, Mr. Brown came right out to see me. He didn't even say hello. It was about eleven o'clock in the morning. He said, "Can you make the four o'clock train for

Cleveland? For the leading spot, twelve weeks, in Robert McLaughlin's company. The first play is *Lost Sheep*. It opens Monday night."

That was in four days. I said, "How come so little notice?" He replied, "I can't take the time to explain. It's a great opportunity. They have a star system in the company. Every week an important star from Broadway comes down. When a male star is playing, the leading woman has a choice of any female part. When a woman star is there, you can choose any part except hers." He added, "As the permanent leading woman you will have a tremendous chance to act. I'll give you the script of *Lost Sheep* so you can study it on the way. The part is the one Sydney Fox played on Broadway." I replied, "Oh, yes. I've seen it." He said, "Good," but I thought, Oh God, me following Sydney Fox was wild. She was half my size and looked fourteen years old.

I asked, "Mr. Brown, tell me the truth. Would any girl who walked through this door have gotten the job?" He said, "Not exactly. The girl had to be ready for this kind of responsibility. And you are." I then asked, "One more question. Who *was* going to play the part and disappointed you at the last minute?" He answered, "Ruth Gordon." "Oh!" I said, "I'll be on the four o'clock train." I thought that I couldn't pass up this chance to replace Ruth Gordon.

On the train I read the script of *Lost Sheep*—about a clergyman with a wife and three daughters who had rented a house that had been a brothel. It was a very funny comedy involving the young men who mistook the daughters for ladies of the night. I was to play the most innocent daughter who discovered at the end of the first act that "There's more to kissing than that!" She was supposed to be a petite teen-ager. There's an old theater cliche that says an actress has to be middle-aged and seasoned before she can play Juliet. As I read the script, I thought with alarm that with my mature figure and deep voice it would take a slight miracle, or at least a tremendous dramatic effort on my part, to convince the audience that I was an innocent little thing.

But that's what acting is about. During rehearsals in

Cleveland, I had literally to transform myself into another generation, and raise my voice an octave. The director was not very happy the first day and almost quit when he took one look at me. But Robert McLaughlin had faith in me, and I surprised everybody with my performance.

So they weren't terribly worried when I took on my next assignment as the delicate, ethereal Grazia in *Death Takes a Holiday*. That's how I came to play leading roles later, in *Blessed Event*, *The Tavern*, *Rain*, and other plays opposite stars like Thomas Mitchell, Franchot Tone, Ernest Glendinning, Lee Tracy, Jane Cowl, and Ina Claire.

When I finished that summer, Robert McLaughlin did me the honor of inviting me back for the 1932 season the following year. I was delighted. I felt secure as an actress, and considered myself really professional. If Father could only see me.

I occasionally thought about Jed. I was spurred on to work and study, to become perfect in my chosen craft. Subconsciously, I was trying to show him what a special girl he had let down.

Voracious reading was still my hobby and my pleasure. Books continued to be my escape. I didn't mind working most of my waking hours. I didn't know that I was preparing for my role as a future liberated workaholic.

By the second season I was ready to demonstrate my strength of character and determination to be totally in command of my life and body—and so I thought—free.

I still equated sex with love and a desire to be as close as possible to someone I admired and loved. The thought of just satisfying my physical lust never entered my mind. The experience with Jed, plus my uninspiring relationship with Irving, made it very difficult for me to let myself go. I worked too hard to allow my dates to get intimate or close. I was very adept at keeping my relationships at an intellectual level. Maybe I just wasn't awakened sexually.

CHAPTER ELEVEN

The World Was Mine

THE DECADE of the 30's was the most tumultuous and far-reaching in American history. It was the time of the Depression, the start of World War II, the beginning of social welfare and reform, a renaissance in the arts, medicine, the physical sciences, the birth of commercial aviation and trans-oceanic flight, radio and television, greater independence for women, and growing rebellion against academic and religious institutions. The decade began with the collapse of the world money markets. Auden's "low dishonest decade" produced the profoundest changes in thinking and feeling, in manners, speech, and dress.

That winter and spring (1931–32) back in New York, I managed to keep going, despite a jobless husband, the Depression, and Father's grave illness. The country was going through hell, and Roosevelt's attempt to alleviate economic and social problems gave us all new sets of initials to live with—WPA, NRA, CCC. I was barely aware of the terrible problems plaguing the rest of the world as I tried to survive in my own private domain.

My sister Rosalie was a little past sixteen—an awkward, sensitive age for any girl—and too heavy. She clung to Father just as

I had before her. Lucy was only twelve, too young to remember the privation and horror of her first three years, and barely able to realize the gravity of Father's illness. Mother, in her incompetency, was in a total daze. She was certainly not equipped to run his business. Her accomplishment as a saleswoman derived from her talent for looking pretty, acting coquettish, and, when necessary, telling her sad story. Was there a moral value to her suffering? Did it help her cope? I wonder.

I resumed my several jobs—night club engagements, my radio program, and my *Morning Telegram* column—to keep Irving and me in reasonable comfort. For my column I dug up gossipy, harmless tidbits, mixed with observations of the New York scene:

Sophie Tucker has left us again. This time for Capone City. . . . Corinne Griffith and her husband, Walter Morosco, spent a weekend with the Prince of Wales at his country estate. . . . A girl in one of our revues has just left the cast on account of illness, but she didn't say that it was husband-fist trouble. . . . Somebody's laughing very quietly at Theodore Dreiser these days. Theodore took it into his head to sue Horace Liveright for a small sum, as a matter of principle, and then discovered that he owed Horace three thousand dollars. Liveright has it all figured out how he will spend it if he ever collects. . .

I got to see the shows because producers in those days were generous with passes and very few plays were sold out. That gave actors a chance to see almost everything that was playing. Since I was a part-time columnist in addition, it was especially easy for me to get tickets. And, of course, we actors had to cover the producers' offices regularly, so—to kill two birds with one stone—we asked for passes and reminded them of our existence.

Just before going on the road with *Topaze*, I had made a screen test with 20th Century-Fox. The man in charge, Rufus LaMaire, was not exactly a diplomat. After the test was finished, he told me I would never get anywhere in movies because I had "a lousy profile." So that spring, when I got a call from MGM, my hopes were not very high. Lewis Milestone, a Russian director, and Ben Piazza, the 300-pound jovial giant who was then the MGM casting director, had come East, I was told, to find an unknown for the role of Sadie Thompson in the remake of *Rain*.

I knew that gag. Usually they had already picked out a star, but a good stunt was to have a publicity campaign "to discover an unknown." So, when they called me, because I had just been studying the part of Sadie, I decided to have the pleasure of telling them I was not interested in making any more tests. I had decided that if this medium didn't want me, I didn't want it.

It was a nice sunny afternoon as the two moguls from Hollywood sat in Al Altman's office patronizingly explaining what a great opportunity this was for a young actress. That was all I needed. I looked Mr. Milestone in the eye and said: "I don't need you to judge whether I can play Sadie Thompson. I have proof I can. I don't know how good I would be in the movies, but surely you'll never find out from the kind of tests you make in New York. I'm an actress in the theater. I've proven it, and I know it. Obviously, I'm not screen material from the tests I've made for Metro Goldwyn and others in the past. Thank you very much for asking me, and I hope you'll find your unknown. But, if you don't, you'll have a roster of stars who could probably do it. So, good luck." (As it happened, the movie came out six months later, starring Joan Crawford, so it probably had already been completed when they invited me to make the test.)

When I got downstairs and walked through the revolving door of the Loew's State Building, I ran into a handsome, young actor I knew whose name was Milton LeRoy. He asked me what I was doing there, and I proudly told him of the speech I made. He said wistfully, "How lucky can you be? I'm dying to get a test, and no one has offered me one."

Suddenly, I realized I could help him. I said, "Come with me, Milton. I have an idea." And up we went, back to the Al Altman office. When I told my friend Marian Landsman my idea, she thought it was great. She buzzed Mr. Milestone and told him that I was back and asked if he could see me for a minute. When I faced Mr. Milestone I said, "If I may choose my scene and my leading man, I will reconsider your offer and make the test." He approved and we made the appointment for the following morning. Then he asked: "Would you mind telling me what scene you are going to do and who your leading man is?" I answered, "I'd rather not, if you don't mind. I'd like it to be a surprise, and it's a good one, believe me." He said, "Okay, I trust your judgment. I like your spirit."

That night, Milton and I stayed up learning the scene from a play called *Cynara*. It was a heartbreaking scene for the girl, very potent, played with an English accent. The man was handsome and a little cold although very charming. He was throwing her over, and she was trying to comprehend this tragedy, just before she commits suicide.

We showed up at the Fox Studio on 10th Avenue, to make the test, and I played it for all the drama and tears I could, spurred on by fear of failure. I had learned the power of my voice by then—I could hold a whole audience with a whisper. Milton upstaged me, of course, by agreement, so that they could see his handsome face. We finished, shook hands, made a $50 bet on who would get the first contract to Hollywood, and said goodbye.

I won the bet. He didn't make it till two years after me. But he changed his name to Philip Reed and stayed in pictures longer than I did. I went on the road, and the last few months of touring with *Topaze* convinced me that the theater was my life.

A couple of weeks before I was to leave for Cleveland, I was gathering material for my last few columns and went to see William Brady in his office on top of the Playhouse Theater on East 48th Street. It was early in April 1932, and I wanted to see a play he had running on Broadway by Adela Rogers St. John, *A Free Soul*, the story of her father. It was a lovely day outside when

I went into the dark hallway to take the skimpy, creaky elevator to the top floor. I almost dreaded seeing the old man. He was over six foot three, had a large body and a pot belly with a gold chain across it. He wore wrinkled clothes that looked as if he had slept in them, and he reeked of liquor. I had never worked for him, but there was always hope. He was an important producer, father of Alice Brady and the husband of Florence George, impressive stars. Brady played the starring role in *A Free Soul*. By now, much as I hated it, sparring with producers and trying to keep as far as possible from them were part of the price, I realized, for being in the swim. There was always the hope that I would get to be important enough to tell them to go to hell. But meantime, I sparred.

After a couple of minutes of polite pleasantries, Brady told me how much he enjoyed my column, called me a smart girl, and promised to keep me in mind for the right part in a future play. Moreover, he didn't even make a tiny pass that morning. Maybe I was getting my message across, or maybe another young girl had been there before me and the old buzzard had had a go with her. On my way out, his secretary gave me a written order for the box office, and I sailed out of the office, pleased with myself, my head high.

The area outside the office was a dark, small landing with one window at the end that barely permitted enough light to see the elevator button. I don't believe the window had been washed in twenty years. I pushed the button and heard the familiar creak of the elevator as it labored up the four flights. Suddenly, from the fire stairs next to the elevator, there came the most beautiful, melodious, cultured voice, slightly breathless, saying, "How foolish not to remember that this old theater had an elevator! It serves me right. I do hope Mr. Brady is in."

I couldn't see the face of the man. He didn't look very tall, but I was instantly fascinated by his voice. I said, "You're in luck. Mr. Brady is in." And to stall for time, I added, "Your voice sounds very familiar; do I know you?" He chuckled and said, "I don't know, but so does yours, and very distinctive. The only way we can solve it is to walk over to that dirty window and see each other's faces."

I stepped over to the window and stood there with my back to the light as he faced me. There before me was Douglas MacLean, "The Prince of Hollywood," with the friendliest smile and the most beautiful row of teeth I had ever seen. Movie star, super-producer, elegant, poised, successful. Even in the dark and dingy hall, you could tell from his bearing that he was used to making public appearances. All I could blurt out was, "I know who you are!" He answered, "This isn't fair; you must turn around so I can see your face." We changed places, and, as the light illuminated my face, he said, "I know who you are. I was in Philadelphia visiting my sister when you were playing there in *Topaze*. I hadn't seen the play in New York. It was your closing week. I am so glad I saw it—you were excellent."

That was the beginning of a beautiful day. He asked me what I was doing and remarked that I was pretty enough to be in pictures. I told him that I was not acting at the moment but writing a column and getting ready to go to Cleveland for three months to play stock. He seemed impressed when I mentioned the column. He told me that he always called on William Brady to pay his respects when he was in New York because he had played for him twenty years before, opposite Alice Brady. I asked him if he would mind my mentioning our meeting in my column. He surprised me by saying, "Of course you can mention that, but I'll do even better. I'm scheduled to leave for the Coast tomorrow morning, but, if I can change it for the next day, will you have lunch with me tomorrow and I'll give you a real interview? I have to check with my office." I gave him my phone number, and he promised to let me know the next morning. I didn't sleep much that night. It was about 9:30 a.m. when he called to say he was sorry he had to leave, but he made me promise that when I got to Hollywood (which he said was inevitable), to please look him up.

There was something in this man's manner and speech that

made an indelible impression on me. He was the most elegant man I had ever met. I didn't identify with him in the girl-and-boy sense. He was too far away, on a pedestal, completely out of reach. I would have felt the same way if he had been the Prince of Wales.

Soon after that, it was time to leave for Cleveland. I went to Brooklyn with a heavy heart to say goodbye to Father. His skin was scarred with radium burns. He was in agony, and, when I saw him, he had been given a dose of morphine. He lay in his bed at home, stoic in his private hell. His tongue was so hideously swollen that he couldn't talk at all, but he smiled bravely at me and wrote a note: "Look after Mother, my Princess. I hope she will find a nice man. Make the best of everything."

My grief was so deep that I could only pray he wouldn't suffer too long. Poor Rosalie had the job of nursing him. She learned to give him the morphine injections and watched him disintegrate. And I escaped the agony of watching him die.

When I returned to Cleveland that season, I was received with open arms. The press milked the story of our escape from Russia and gave me very good notices. I remained good copy. Robert McLaughlin was a wonderful, kind producer, a joy to work for. His concern when he learned about my father was terribly important to me. This second season I was given the deference, billing, and treatment of a star. In return, I did everything I could to show my appreciation. The press in Cleveland was wonderful; reviewers and reporters had decided the year before that they liked me. I felt at home and accepted as part of a team. I will always remember that city with affection.

Russell Barnett Aitken, Cleveland's young painter and sculptor, who was doing unusual caricatures in glazed clay, decided to do a sculpture of me as the character of Sadie in *Rain*. I was wined, dined, and invited everywhere and tried to do as much as was humanly possible. But a stock company engagement is grueling work—rehearsing one play for a week during the day and playing another at night. Saturday is a matinee day and Sunday is a dress rehearsal for the following opening on Monday. We worked from 11:00 a.m. to 11:00 p.m. every day and studied our parts in between. Only after the show, and not very often, did I go out socially. When I did, it was with a young professor who had a crush on me and was giving me driving lessons in a new Packard.

After one tiring summer day in June, the 17th to be exact, a gang of us went to a pub after the show to get something to eat. I ordered steak tartare and raw onion, which I thought would help me get a good night's sleep. I couldn't explain a feeling of apprehension and a jumpy spasm in my stomach. I couldn't get my thoughts away from my father and his agonizing pain. I doubted that he even understood me the last time I saw him when I told him about the golden opportunity I was facing in Cleveland. It was midnight when I decided to make a long-distance call to my mother. I heard the phone ring about three times and suddenly Mother's voice. She didn't say hello. She just said, "How did you know?" While I stood there stunned, a steel vise clutched my gut. She told me he was to be buried the next day.

There was no sense in my trying to go to the funeral. It was an overnight trip; I couldn't get there in time. She told me that I wouldn't have been able to see him even in his casket. He had shrunk to ninety pounds, she said, and I was lucky not to have seen him in his last days of agony. Devastated by the realization that I would never see my father again, I hung up the receiver and walked back to my table in a daze. My companions knew by the expression on my face why I couldn't eat. To this day, when I look at steak tartare I relive that telephone call.

The theater tradition that the show must go on was tested then. I had six weeks more to do. There was no understudy for me, and it would have been useless to throw the whole company out of work when there was nothing I could do for Father. The best I could do for Mother was to become as successful as possible. I was filled with guilt that I was not there at the end, but, as much as I loved Father, the devastating thought kept

coming back to me that he had died for me the last time I saw
him. He was so drugged that I didn't think he knew me. It was
guilt and relief at the same time. Even now, my throat fills with a
lump and my eyes with tears whenever I think of him, which is
often. That night, back in my hotel, I made a resolution that I
would try to live up to all his expectations of me.

During that hectic summer I had forgotten the screen test I
had made in New York with Milton LeRoy; I'd never seen it and
didn't care. But a couple of weeks after my father died, Marian
Landsman called me and, in a hushed voice, said, "We have
word from Irving Thalberg." She spoke as if she were talking
about God. "He said he thought you were terrific!"

As I listened to Marian's words, my mind was saying, "Am I
dreaming? This is crazy. I'll wake up and find it's a dream." But
there was Marian going on to explain, "But he wasn't pleased
with the photography of your face and wants just a photographic silent test." I came out of shock and heard myself
saying, "Marian, impossible! Without my voice, I'm nothing."
She said, "Wait a minute. If they ever found out what I'm telling
you, I'd be fired, but here's my idea. You will probably hear from
Al Altman, and he will ask you for the test. Tell him that you'll
be happy to make it . . . but you want it done at MGM in
Hollywood, with Harry Boquet and Bill Daniels—Garbo's test
director and cameraman—a gown by Adrian, and your train fare
and expenses paid for one month. You'll give them your time for
nothing, but the tests must be made in Hollywood where they
know how to photograph actresses. Goodbye and good luck."

The next day, I got the call as she had predicted. I made the
speech she prescribed, and, to my surprise, within a couple of
days, it was all set. After finishing my engagement in stock, I
would go to Hollywood, that mythical actors' heaven, where you
sit in a projection room or theater and see yourself on the screen,
blown up eight times larger than life.

I wrote to my husband and asked him to look around for a
small apartment to live in by himself, or to go back to his family,

since I couldn't any longer afford to pay for our New York apartment while I was away. Secretly, despite my natural optimism, I felt that my chances for fame in Hollywood were not a possibility.

The season ended the last week in July, and McLaughlin gave me a going-away party at the Madrid, a night club. Newspapermen, the cast, the crew, and a few outside friends were there. Everyone was excited because I was on my way to Hollywood. There was much toasting and wishing me well. I developed a slight toothache, but, like a determined actress, behaved as if I had never felt better.

My toothache got worse, even though I took a couple of drinks to ease the pain. I didn't want to spoil the fun, so I told everyone I had to leave early—it was after midnight—in order to catch an early train. Among the guests was a dentist, a friend of one of the crew, who had an office around the corner. I decided to mention my throbbing tooth to him on my way out, and he said, "Come with me. I'll fix you up in ten minutes." The assistant director came with me to the dentist's office. The excitement, liquor and persistent pain were making me very tired. In the dentist's chair I leaned my head back as he put a gas mask over my face. It never occurred to me that he might have had too much to drink and could probably hurt me. I felt myself slipping away in the nirvana of the gas as I heard him say, "This tooth will never hurt you again. I'll fix it." When I came to, he had pulled out one of my important lower molars, a perfectly healthy tooth and with it a piece of my jawbone. The pain I was feeling came from a small leaking cavity in the next tooth (as I learned later). Now, it was excruciating. It was a miracle that I made the train for Chicago the next morning, where I was to board the Super Chief for Hollywood.

I made my changes in Chicago in a daze. My jaw was swollen, and I was miserable. I had a ticket for a lower berth. My luggage was sparse so it was not too much trouble to settle myself into a seat. I tried to think about my arrival in Hollywood. I had written to my friend, William Wyler, who promised to meet me at the train. I knew a few other people in Hollywood already. My jaw was throbbing so I couldn't get comfortable. Closing my eyes, I concentrated on what lay ahead in Hollywood. The thought of my big chance, as well as the conviction that I was ready for it, helped me through the first couple of hours. When I opened my eyes, I was conscious of an athletic young man sitting opposite me. He was watching me and gave me a shy smile. I judged him to be about twenty, a typical clean-cut, lean, blond New England WASP. I was in no mood for conversation so I closed my eyes again and tried to doze, holding a small icebag to my swollen jaw. When the ice melted and I opened my eyes again, the young athlete asked if there was anything he could do for me, and I flippantly replied, "Order me a new jaw." He laughed, then almost blushed and said, "I am sorry. I didn't mean to laugh at you, but you were funny." I blurted out that I was going to Hollywood for my big chance in the movies and how much it all meant to me, particularly how after my father's death when my mother and two two sisters needed me. Baron— that was the fellow's name—listened to me spellbound. He kept asking me questions, and, in my misery, I answered them. By the time we were ready to go to the dining car, I had acquired a slave: twenty-two years old, recently graduated from Yale, on his first business trip, sent by his father to look over the family's vast interests and national offices in Los Angeles and San Francisco. This young man with impeccable manners, shy and sensitive, seemed much younger than his years. He was to the manor born, brought up in a social and sheltered life between Newport and New York. Everything unpleasant happening in the world only happened to the people outside his world. I didn't think that he had ever met anyone in person who had any struggle, drama, or strife and had to fight for survival. I felt so vulnerable and alone in my pain that this gentle young man had no problem getting me to spill my fears and desires. Before I knew it, in his quiet way, he had taken charge of me for the rest of the trip.

The train made a couple of stops along the way—I don't know

what for and they weren't for very long. Baron gave orders and got things done. At one stop he had the engineer of the train order ahead to have someone meet the train on the following stop with proper pain relief, a poultice, and a hot water bag. Evidently my icebag was the wrong thing to apply. He also ordered all my food cut up and soups and juices for the rest of the trip. He treated me like a helpless injured puppy, and I loved it.

Baron told me about himself. I learned about his family and his upbringing, how his life was programmed for him and that there was no question but that he would follow his parents' planning. He told me he was going to be in Los Angeles for two days, leaving on the second day for San Francisco, where he expected to be three or four days, and then he would go back to New York. A beautiful friendship would end after one day in Hollywood.

When we arrived there, Willie Wyler met me at the train as promised. He gave me a little box containing a small, uncut gold key, a symbol of the key to Hollywood. I knew where I was going to stay. The Ravenswood on Vine Street was rented for me by MGM for one month. Baron was met by someone from his office. Thus we said our "so longs" on the train before we got off, but we had made a dinner date for the first night, his only night in Los Angeles. Willie drove me to the Ravenswood, explaining along the way that he was sorry that he couldn't see me because he was involved in a love affair.

I wasn't in the apartment one hour when the phone rang and Baron asked me if I would go with him to help pick out a car. He said he thought he might drive to San Francisco. My jaw was better but still very tender, and I thought it would be fun to go shopping for a car. He picked me up in a taxi, and we rode to the Cord showroom on Wilshire Boulevard. Baron thought that I should look over the situation now and get acquainted with the type of car I might want in the future. I said he was being premature. When we got to the showroom, my eyes riveted on a pearl-gray Cord roadster. It was the most graceful and smashing car I had ever seen. I don't remember the price exactly, but it was exorbitant and impossible for me at the time. Baron asked, "Would you like this?" And I replied, "You remind me of Marie Antoinette when she was told that the people had no bread and her answer was, 'Let them eat cake.' " Baron laughed. I think I made him laugh twice, and I wonder if he laughed much in his life.

He decided to buy the roadster that I liked, wrote a check for it, and arranged to drive it right out of the showroom. The car was filled with gasoline, and he drove me around Los Angeles a bit in this stunning roadster before dropping me off at the Ravenswood. He was staying at the Ambassador and suggested that we have dinner in the Coconut Grove. We had a lovely evening, and he brought me home early. My jaw was very sore. I was due at MGM the next morning and a good night's rest was very important. He never gave me his New York address, but he knew where I was. I did see Baron twice after that—for lunch at Sardi's in New York five years later in 1937 and the last time in Palm Beach in 1975, just before he died.

As I came down into the lobby of the Ravenswood, there was a note in my box instructing me to see the garage attendant on the level below. I thought that the driver of the MGM car must be waiting for me there. The garageman handed me an envelope on which was written, "To Barbara. Best wishes and good luck. May this take you where you want to go." Signed "B." I tore open the envelope. It was the registration to the Cord roadster in my name, all paid for.

I was so flabbergasted, I didn't know what to say. In my stupor, I showed it to the MGM driver who said, "Nice present. Do you have a driver's license?" I answered that I did not. He offered to take me to get one after my first appointment. The driver was in on Baron's little drama and thought it was sensational, and so did I. There was no way I could reach Baron to thank him, but if there is any truth in ESP, he must have gotten my thoughts and messages.

Baron's magnanimous gift, with no strings attached, was a

gesture that staggered me and reaffirmed my belief in God and my good fortune. I couldn't help wondering what had prompted this young man—in many ways worldly and sophisticated, in other ways so innocent and protected from the seamier things in life—to give me such an expensive gift. There was such a difference in our lives. He didn't want anything from me and never expected to see me after we said goodbye. All he said was, "Good luck. I know I'll be seeing you on the screen." He kissed me on the cheek and vanished.

My mind was racing as I was driven to my first appointment at MGM. We drove through Beverly Hills, across town, past Fox Studio to Culver City. As we neared the vast studio complex that seemed like miles of white-washed wall, I saw the impressive black, iron double gate with the police stationed at each side. It looked like a fortress. My driver slowed down and stopped; the guard pressed a button that opened an enormous gate; and I was driven onto the lot like in a real movie.

What an omen! The shiny, graceful Cord roadster waiting for me—all mine—and this entrance to MGM had to mean a happy ending. My heart was bursting with thankfulness and love.

Mother and Father after their wedding in New York in 1906.

Mother, Father and I when I was six months old. This is the last picture taken of us before we left for Russia in 1908.

Ovcei, Mother and Father.

Grandmother, as she looked in 1902 before I was born.

Grandfather, Father and Abraham.

Mother and I when I was almost seven, after she came back from Paris with her first haircut and I got one to match. I had on my first French dress.

Lucy and her nurse in 1919 just before we left Zhitomir.

My U.S. passport picture.

My first home in America. It was the pits! The two rooms were filthy and depressing. We lived there six months and then moved upstairs next door. I went back and photographed it in 1959 and it looked exactly the same as I had remembered it.

My first school, P.S. 179, was beautiful—I hated to go home to the "hell hole" behind the store.

Our first kitchen, U.S.A.

November 1927, first family portrait in America. I had returned first class on the Paris and I was on Broadway five years after Ellis Island.

Father bought this house at 1870 East 55th St., Brooklyn, in 1926. I lived there four years until 1930 and Mother lived there until 1935. It was sold in 1940 by Rosalie when they all came to California to live permanently.

Jed Harris, my first big
mistake.

Shubert-Belasco
The Theatre Beautiful of Washington City
A Playhouse of Quality and Personality Presenting
The Foremost Foreign and Native Artists and
Attractions of the Speaking Stage

Direction Lee and J. J. Shubert

L. Stoddard Taylor, Mgr.

Sept 24th '27

My Dear Friend Hoover:—

Will you if nothing
prevents to day, kindly
let Mrs Barondess of
our company have a
look over the White House.
Mrs Barondess is
playing her first engagement
in Washington and would
much appreciate the courtesy.
Kindest regards
Sincerely yours
LS Taylor

Not merely what we do, but what we try to do and why, are the true interpreters of what we are

The letter to Herbert Hoover
that got me into the White
House in September 1927.

An impression done while I
was appearing as Ernestine
Muche in "Topaze."

I pose for sculptor Russell
Barnett Aitkin while
appearing in "Death Takes
a Holiday" in Cleveland.

In 1927, I (center) appeared
at the Selwyn Theater,
42nd St., in "The Garden
of Eden" with Alison
Skipworth and
Mirriam Hopkins.

When I met Douglas, I was wearing these clothes, my version of what a journalist should look like.

A real Prince Charming — my second husband, Douglas MacLean, whom I met in 1932 and married in 1936 — silent movie star and Paramount producer.

The frame from my Hollywood screen test made while I was in "Topaze."

I witness the ceremony in "Hold Your Man" with Jean Harlow and Clark Gable.

"Rasputin and the Empress" starred the three Barrymores. Here I am (at left) with Lionel Barrymore.

In 1926 I was the maid in "The Plot Thickens" with Zazu Pitts and Jimmy Gleason.

"The Maxim Girls"—I am with Maurice Chevalier, God's gift to women.

I am photographed with Ernst Lubitsch.

"The Merry Widow," 1934
—me, Jeanette McDonald and
Maurice Chevalier.

"Easy Money"–
Onslow Stevens and
me.

In 1934 I (at left) play with Baby
Peggy in "Eight Girls in a Boat."

Regis Toomey admires my
jewelry in "Soldiers of the
Storm," in 1933 with
Anita Page.

At the age of 27, I have the title role in "Her Majesty the Prince" at the Music Box Theater in Los Angeles.

When I played in "Pursuit of Happiness" with Mary Boland and Joan Bennett, I worked on the set on my "Hollywood Reporter" column. As a reporter, I trailed Gretta Garbo and ended up acting with her as Elsa, a countrygirl maid, in "Queen Christina."

The Screen Actors Guild was born in 1934 and I (front car) played in "Change of Heart" with James Dunn, Ginger Rogers, Charles Farrell, Janet Gaynor, and Kenneth Thompson.

Barbara Barondess,
James Dunn, Anita
Loos at MGM gate
in '34.

Broadway play by Arthur Kober (Lillian Hellman's husband), "Lady Be Careful," became
a Paramount picture. I played with Lew Ayres, Mary Carlisle, Buster Crabbe, Benny
Baker and Grant Withers.

Lucy, Rosalie and I as we posed in Hollywood in 1937.

Publicity pictures were taken of me in clothes I designed in 1933-34.

North Palm, our first home, with my name on the deed. My dream house!

Mrs. Douglas MacLean — no bleached hair — I'm playing my favorite part.

The MacLeans with the engineer on their yacht, the Comrade — My cup runneth over.

CHAPTER TWELVE

Off the Ground and in Orbit

MY FIRST appointment on the lot was in the office of its
casting director, Ben Piazza. His secretary was a small
Irish girl named Florence Barton, about five feet tall, with a pert
little face, mousey brown hair, and a turned-up nose. She
greeted me warmly and ushered me into Mr. Piazza's office. This
large hulk of a man was again very friendly. He chuckled as he
said, "All your demands have been met. William Daniels will
photograph your test. Harry Boquet is going to direct it. He's
Garbo's test director. Florence will take you over to Wardrobe
now and you'll be fitted in an Adrian gown." He added, "Eight
o'clock tomorrow morning be at the make-up department and
then the hairdresser's after that. Our test is scheduled for 10
a.m. Good luck."

Florence took me for a short tour of the MGM Studio. My first
impression was that I was on a street with enormous white-
washed warehouses, like barracks that had been evacuated.
There was an eerie unreality in the air. The buildings were

designated Stage 1, Stage 2, etc. Each had a heavy metal door, a red bulb over the top of it, and a sign on the right that said, "Do not enter when the light is on." Florence explained that each sound stage held the sets of a current picture, and that when the red light was on they were shooting a scene. Anyone opening a door then could cost the studio a fortune for the ruined take. This was much more complicated and sophisticated than the old studios in New York. Silent and empty, it was awesome.

Before taking me to Wardrobe, Florence showed me a row of one- and two-story bungalows that held the featured players' and stockplayers' dressing rooms, and big dressing rooms for all the extras; then the buildings that housed the big movie stars. Some were attached and detached bungalows; most had a parking space in front. The super stars were the only ones privileged to drive onto the lot, except, of course, the important producers and directors. The rest of the many hundreds of employees at MGM had to park in the outside parking lot. We didn't have time to go to the fabulous and famous twenty acres of permanently built cities and streets that were called "the Back lot" until later, but I saw the enormous cafeteria-like commissary and was shown the directors' and producers' private dining room.

The Wardrobe department was a large loft, about 300 feet long, where approximately fifty girls sat at sewing machines and tables, mending, sewing, and pressing all kinds of costumes, from the simplest rags to elaborate gowns. It looked like a factory. Each section, divided by a partition, had the name of the picture in front, and groups of girls were assigned to each picture. The wardrobe woman in charge took me over to a special room that said "Adrian, Miscellaneous." It was next to a section filled with elaborate court costumes whose sign read "Rasputin and the Empress." It startled me. Rasputin? Where was I?

After looking over several dresses, I was fitted with a simple V-necked black and white gown. The wardrobe mistress asked me if I wanted a pair of shoes, and I said, "If you have anything large enough. The only ones that might fit me would be Miss

Garbo's." She gave me a look, as if to say, "Not bad; you want to be in Garbo's shoes." How could she know that all I wanted was to check the size so I could win a bet that I had made with Walter Winchell some years before about Garbo's shoe size. Imagine my surprise when I couldn't get her shoes on my feet. Garbo, I found, contrary to Winchell's remark that she had big feet, wore a shoe narrower and a size smaller than mine, and my feet were average.

Although everything in the studio was impressive, tremendous, somehow I had the feeling that I was in a sterile and not very human factory. The emptiness, with the glaring sun of the street outside, depressed me. I think there were five different units making pictures at that time. Although Florence and Ben Piazza and all the people I saw that day were forthcoming and polite, they were terribly impersonal and I felt a little like a number.

Since I didn't have an agent in this whole transaction, and I had met Leo Morrison when he was with the William Morris office in New York, I called and asked him if he would act as my representative, in case something came of this trip. He agreed and invited me to a party at his apartment that evening.

I put on my most demure blue dress—princess style, with tiny buttons covered in the same cornflower blue. The color I was sure of, because Mother and everybody else for years had told me that blue was my color. My swollen jaw was almost normal. I hoped it would be all right for the test the next day. But I still had difficulty chewing. I made an appointment with a local dentist recommended by the studio for the following afternoon. There was so much to do! I had to get my driver's license for I hadn't driven my beautiful car yet!

At Leo's things went smoothly to begin with. He had a girl friend who was called Little Bit. They were both little. One of the guests was Henry Ginsberg, a short, friendly man with a pixie sense of humor who was the head of the Hal Roach Studio. Charles Feldman was another, a lawyer and agent, very sure of himself, good looking, rather tall. He didn't look like a man who would put himself out for anybody, unless it was important to him. And there was Harry Cohn, head of Columbia, perhaps the most disliked man in Hollywood. He was of medium height with an unsmiling face. He was polished, manicured and expensively dressed. He didn't even attempt to be nice, and he never looked you straight in the eye. Before he opened his mouth I knew he was arrogant, and he looked me over as if I were a piece of meat on a butcher counter. I disliked him immediately, and the first thing that flashed in my mind was, "If this is an example of the head of the studio, and what I am up against, God help me!"

Before dinner was over Harry Cohn made several suggestive remarks, asked me if I was a virgin, to which I answered that I was married. He wanted to know if I loved my husband, asked where he was, and was generally obnoxious. Sparring with him was no fun, but I realized I couldn't afford to antagonize him. It was a terrible strain, and I turned to Henry Ginsberg to see if he would join the conversation and help me out of my predicament. He got my cue and started to ask me silly, funny general questions. We got on the subject of herring at Lindy's Restaurant in New York that was the greatest until he came to Hollywood and had some at the Hillcrest Country Club. The subject changed the conversation, and Cohn changed his tactics.

Leo Morrison mentioned my experience in the theater and my engagement in *Topaze* and Mr. Cohn decided, I guess, that I was not just another starlet, and became less overbearing. Starlets were the beautiful, ambitious hopefuls who came to Hollywood in droves. They were called starlets only when they were lucky enough to get a contract at a studio. They usually started at $75.00 a week, and each studio had a stable of anywhere from ten to twenty who were sent to school to study acting, were photographed for publicity stunts, rarely played more than a little bit in a picture, and were generally abused. Very few of them ever made it to stardom. The nasty crack was "They danced on one foot and then the other, and managed to make a living in between." (The only exception that I can think of offhand is Marilyn Monroe, and even she, when she was a starlet at 20th Century-Fox, was used, abused and dropped by her studio after one year.) I privately renamed them "Startlets." The Hollywood moguls divided the women into madonnas or whores.

Messrs. Cohn and Ginsberg both asked to take me home, lucky for me. I was safe. I was dropped at my apartment, said my goodnights, and escaped. You can imagine my surprise the next morning when I received a bouquet of flowers from Harry Cohn, and a case of herring from Henry Ginsberg, with a funny note. I didn't meet Henry Ginsberg again until ten years later, when he was head of Paramount.

I arrived at MGM the next morning, knowing that this was Do or Die day. When I thought about my test, which was to be silent, I was petrified. I tried to tell Harry Boquet that I was an actress, not just a face, and without my voice I couldn't possibly compete with the beauties under contract to MGM. He told me gently that they had seen my New York test and they knew I could act. What they wanted was just a photographic test, front face and profile, for Mr. Thalberg to see. It didn't make sense to me. You had to play something innocent or worldly or young or old or common or educated, and for each character you made a different face. He was sorry but his orders were to make a silent test. I was disappointed as I sat on a chair in front of the camera and turned my face to the left and then to the right, looked into the camera, a blank. Suddenly it was over.

On the way back to Piazza's office, I thought of the agonizing time of waiting in Poland and then in England; the fear that we would not get to America, and then the two weeks at Ellis Island waiting to be allowed to land—and now I was at the end of the line still waiting—for approval, to be able to stay in Hollywood and work. Would I always be dependent on some unknown person to pull the strings of my fate? Terror clutched my stomach. Here I was a month past twenty-five. It was ten years since we had arrived in America.

In Piazza's office right after, I told Florence how I dreaded the results of that test becaue it was silent. She tried to reassure me and promised she would try to get me a look at my test. She called one of the projectionists and asked him to show it to me the next morning at 8:30, before anybody else saw it. The projection room was booked for nine o'clock for the directors to look at my rushes they had shot the day before.

I made up my mind that if I didn't look good in this test, I wasn't going to stick around and put my emotions and my hopes through a wringer. I would pack up and go home. I wasn't very happy when I got to the dentist, who looked at my jaw and shook his head. He asked, "Who did this to you, a butcher?" The rest of the day and evening were a sad blur. I did get my driver's license. Because the studio had pull, I didn't even have to take a driving test.

I was up at the crack of dawn, excited to be driving my beautiful new car in the empty streets, arrived at MGM in time for a cup of coffee in the commissary, then walked to the projection room. It was dark. I sat on the left about halfway down front. There were buttons and a device that looked like a microphone in front of my chair, which had a wooden tray that swung back from the arms, for the purpose of taking notes. I pushed the button, heard a voice from the projection room, and said, "I am Barbara Barondess and I'm here to see a test."

The man said, "Okay," and started to roll. Strangely enough with all the silent movies I had been in and the bits that I had played, I had not seen myself on the screen, except once after I won the beauty contest and saw the Fox newsreel, and then I thought I looked awful in the striped swimsuit. Now I was looking at a girl in a close-up that filled the large screen eight times larger than life, just silently sitting there with a wistful expression, who turned to the right and then to the left. As I was watching I heard voices, and several people walked into the projection room right in the middle of the showing. I slid down in my seat and someone buzzed the projectionist, saying in a thick Russian accent, "Run that again." Then he said to somebody, "Charlie, Ben, take a look at this girl." I couldn't hear what they were saying, but they were talking through the rerun. When it was over for the second time, the man with the Russian accent asked the projectionist if there was any talking film on this actress. "Yes, a New York test." I slumped lower in my seat, trying not to be discovered, and for the first time saw the scene I had done in New York with Milton Le Roy, "Philip Reed."

When it was over I heard one of the men say, "We've got our girl. You're right, Bole, no sense looking at the other tests." They all got up and left as suddenly as they had entered.

Astonished and fearful, I sneaked out of the room as quickly as I could and went to look for Florence. When I told her what had happened, she said, "Barbara, you sure are lucky! Those men were Richard Boleslavsky, Charles MacArthur, Ben Hecht, and Bernie Hyman, producer. They're all connected with *Rasputin and the Empress*. Remember, we saw some costumes being made for it? It's going to star the three Barrymores—Lionel, John, and Ethel."

"God," I said. "If it's true, what a way to start!" Boleslavsky was the hero director, former assistant to Russian guru Stanislavsky.

Rasputin was the only movie in which all three Barrymores appeared together. Lionel had the title role, and I was to play several scenes with him. Ethel was the Empress, and John was Prince Felix Yusupov who killed Rasputin.

Within three days the Hollywood *Reporter* announced that I had joined the cast. I met Bernie Hyman, the producer, director Richard Boleslavsky, and writers Ben Hecht and Charles Mac-Arthur (whose wife, Helen Hayes, was making *A Farewell to Arms* with Gary Cooper). I was formally introduced to Publicity Department head Howard Strikling, sent to Wardrobe, given a script of four or five pages, and told where and when to report for the first day's shooting.

All I could tell from the script was that I had some dialogue with Rasputin and that there were several other people in the scene. There was no description of my character and there was no name for her. It just said, "Miss Barondess," to indicate which lines were mine.

I could learn nothing from Boleslavsky except that I was a sidekick or girl friend of Rasputin's and that I would be at his side whenever he was shown at a gathering or at a party. Was this how the renowned Hollywood professionals made films?

It was pure chance they had happened to come fifteen minutes earlier than scheduled and had seen my test. Was all the work and preparation needed only for a chance to be in the right place at the right time? I wondered if it was coincidence or fate. Strange too that the picture was about Rasputin and that I'd spent ten years learning to speak English without the trace of an accent only to be cast as a Russian in my first talking movie. They gave me no clue as to the characterization of the part. Who was I supposed to be—a peasant, a commoner, middle class, a duchess? It was up to me to find out.

I gradually learned that this was an unusually disorganized company, and it was a miracle that the film ever got finished—no script except for one day ahead; and three Barrymores, who were tough enough to take individually, together they spelled disaster. John and his temperament, Lionel and his illness (he was in a wheelchair between takes) and Ethel on the wagon. She was a formidable woman. All this was enough to throw any young actress, but not me. This job was my only chance for a movie career, and I was not going to blow it. I decided to be Anna Vyroubova, historically credited with introducing Rasputin to the Empress. In some historical accounts she was a beautiful virgin and in others she was ugly and twice married. I decided to play her down the middle.

My first scene was with Lionel Barrymore and Diana Wynyard, a lovely English actress playing the part of Princess Irina Yusupov. In the scene she calls on Rasputin at his house while he's having a dinner party. I am sitting next to him. When she comes in he gets up from the table while I glower. He takes her hand, and with obvious lecherous intentions escorts her to a bedroom door. I get up to follow as he opens the door and is surprised by a beautiful blonde, her long hair covering her partially disrobed body, waiting for him. Rasputin goes to the next bedroom, which he finds empty, escorts Irina Yusupov into it, and closes the door. I am supposed to be blind with rage and burst into hysterical laughter.

What a start for an actress! I rehearsed the scene without a hitch. But the strong kleig lights were killers. They were blinding and very hot, and the confinement of the chalk marks for the camera were something new to me. The size of the stage, the crew, soundmen, property men, lighting men, make-up men, hairdressers, script girls, and dozens of assistants, photographers, and all those people fussing and stopping every shot were absolutely devastating. The lights bothered me the most. I was sure that I would photograph blind. Registering rage and hysteria in the second scene not difficult! I heard my cue, "Roll!"

I threw myself into the part with such abandon that I completely forgot the camera and where I was. By the time the shots rang out indicating Rasputin's death by assassination I was living, not acting, my role as the crazed monk's intimate friend and advisor. I tried to stifle a scream and could not stop a hysterical cry, when I heard: CUT!

A big, shaggy man wrapped something around me and led me to a chair. I could not stop shaking and whimpering. Someone handed me a glass of water. The man kept his arm about my shoulders. It was calming, reassuring and warm. He bent down and I was looking into the eyes of the great Russian director, Richard Boleslavsky. He whispered, "*Horosho*, very good. You made me believe that we were there!"

Where was I? At MGM—on stage #10, the set of *Rasputin and the Empress*—my first talking movie, starring John, Lionel, and Ethel Barrymore. I was playing Anna Vyroubova. I had to pinch myself. Was this a dream?

There was something uncanny about my playing in this picture about Rasputin. I felt close to the events, for in 1916, when I was only nine years old in Russia, my family had talked about Rasputin's influence and his threats that if any harm came to him Russia and the Royal Family would go down with him. And, of course, the Royal Family was slaughtered in 1918.

But my wildest dreams then did not encompass that I would travel halfway around the world and be in Hollywood in 1932 to play Anna Vyroubova with the Barrymores, without a Russian accent.

We broke for lunch and I proceeded to the commissary. I had been accepted.

The comissary was jam-packed with actors wearing costumes from every period picture being made on the lot along with the writers and technicians. It was a strange sight. I was wandering around looking for a place to sit down when I heard my name. Bernie Hyman's assistant, Jack Cummings, who was Louis B. Mayer's nephew, was calling me. At his table for eight to ten people was an empty seat, and he motioned me to sit down. As I did, he started to introduce me to the people on my right and went counter-clockwise so I had no chance to look to my left until someone took my hand to shake it, as I turned to say, "How do you do?"—and it stuck in my throat.

I was looking into the bluest eyes I had ever seen; they belonged to Gary Cooper. The shock that went through me made me feel absolutely on fire. He was obviously enjoying the effect he was having on me and still holding my hand, as I heard Jack Cummings' voice bringing me out of my shock. He said, "I don't believe it! You are actually blushing," and I was, right through my make-up.

I had to say something, because Cooper was still holding my hand—so I blurted out without thinking, "You know one Cooper in the hand is worth two Cummings in the bush," and the roar of laughter from everyone at the table was so loud and spontaneous that everyone around turned to look at our table. That crack earned me a reputation of a quick wit, but I felt like a nitwit.

When I realized how suggestive and smartass my remark

was, I got up and bolted to the Ladies Room to pull myself together. After about five minutes I returned to my seat and a normal conversation about what was going on in Hollywood and on Broadway resumed. Cooper had an appointment about fifteen minutes later—I did not see him again for six months—but that is another story.

Later the real Prince Yusupov sued MGM for defiling his wife's image in that suggestive bit, and the company paid him $750.00. The blonde in the first room was played by Francesca Braggiotti, wife of John Davis Lodge, who at the time was making a film about Catherine of Russia, *The Scarlet Empress*, with Marlene Dietrich. Unfortunately, Francesca was completely cut out of the picture, along with most of my scene, because of Yusupov's suit.

Up to this time, no one had said a word to me about salary or contract. I called Leo Morrison, who suggested that I keep my mouth shut. Starlets and beginners received about $75.00 a week—that was minimum. Although my salary in the theater had reached four times as much, I decided that the opportunity to be in this picture and be directed by Boleslavsky, who, besides having been the assistant to the great Stanislavsky, had written a book on acting that became the young actor's Bible, was more important than money.

The theater had been an intimate business. It was easy for everyone in the theater to know each other on Broadway with its couple of dozen productions a season and a couple of hundred actors working. The movie industry was another story. It was a production factory with thousands of actors and twice as many technicians.

I was on the picture for six months and never met Ethel Barrymore because I was never involved in a scene with her. After a picture was finished, it took about six months to a year to prepare it, print, edit and cut for preview. You might meet or see many of the others at the preview.

Everything went smoothly the first few days. Bernie Hyman, the producer, appeared on the set every day and always made a point of coming over to talk to me. I found a chair in the corner, and settled to observe and learn. The waiting between takes was tedious. Every shot was taken from different angles, long, medium, and close-up, and repeated until the director, cameraman, soundman and star were satisfied. That's not allowing for noises, blowing a line, and other mistakes.

It was a dull and exhausting procedure, but I was going to grin and bear it. Every day I prayed the Boleslavsky would give me direction. The most I got from him was "Good morning." I couldn't tell whether I was hopeless or great. I remembered Guthrie; maybe I didn't understand directors.

On Friday we were dismissed and told to go to the cashier to collect the week's salary. I was prepared for the minimum. The line at the cashier's desk was considerable. It was like a factory, but it moved fast as each person announced his name and the title of the picture. Each was handed a sealed envelope. When I got mine, I decided to drive home before opening it. I wanted to savor it, like saving the biggest strawberry for last.

The pleasure of driving my new car with my first week's salary in my pocket inspired a silent prayer to my father. Was it ten years since Ellis Island? It seemed much shorter. Maybe I was on the way?

When I came into the apartment I had only one regret. There was no one to share this with. I made myself some coffee and sat down at the little dining table for the official opening of the envelope. I carefully slit it with a knife, removed the contents, and saw four crisp, new $100 bills, two $20's, and $10. I sat there in a stupor—$450.00? Must be a mistake.

When I got to the studio Monday morning, the assistant director told me my call was at noon so I had time to run to the cashier. When I said that there must have been a mistake, she looked up and said that my salary was $75.00 a day until I finished the part. I didn't know if I should shout with joy or cry.

The picture dragged on for six months, and I didn't go off the payroll until it was finished. No one ever mentioned a contract, although I was treated like a contract player by the Publicity

Department and Casting Office. The only person I could talk to was little Florence in the Casting Office. She told me all the studio gossip. I learned the inside politics, and who was sleeping with whom. Every executive had his puppets and pulled their strings to suit his whims. I confided my anxieties to her. I had no champion at the studio to advise me or give my career a push.

Roles make actors. If you get a good part on the stage, it doesn't matter how short it is, if it's good. Once the curtain goes up, it's the actor and his audience. You are on your own; the applause is your barometer. Acting is a lonely profession because you are admired for being someone else. The most important careers were based on the figment of a writer's imagination. All the biographies one reads prove conclusively how insecure, miserable, and lonely most of the great idols of the stage and screen were, and how vulnerable. They lived in a make-believe world.

Florence gave me a thorough education and told me that to become a star in Hollywood the usual formula required you to get under a good producer and work up. I was scared. The chief, L.B., seemed like a monster. He had a stable of very young, long-legged fillies, mostly jailbait. He was paternal and strict, and the ones who had stage mothers, he had in the palms of his hands.

Number Two was Irving Thalberg, the genius. Thin, sensitive, good-looking and not very robust—actually fragile. He was married to Norma Shearer and did not play around. He was the one who was responsible for my being there. But he never sent for me, and I never met him.

The rest of the important executives with various titles all had their proteges. Eddie Mannix was a big square-jawed man who looked like a tough police sergeant. Harry Rapf was a skinny, dark homely man credited with discovering Joan Crawford. Ben Thaw was a newcomer with a job as head of contract players. A graduate of the William Morris Agency, he later discovered Greer Garson. Then there were Albert Lewin, a very short man, about 5'2", almost albino blond with a translucent quality; Larry Weingarden, married to a sister of Thalberg; Jack Cummings, L.B.'s nephew, insecure, good-looking, self-conscious; Paul Bern, an intellectual, married to Jean Harlow; Bernie Hyman, who looked like the owner of an expensive men's clothing store.

Mostly they were an ugly, bad-tempered, bad-mannered bunch, whose power and money went to their heads. And while they had it, they used it. At this time MGM was the most powerful studio in the world and its stars were the most valuable commodity. They went on a spree of signing up the brightest new talent from the dramatic, literary, and musical worlds. They had struck oil with the talkies and they had Garbo, Crawford, Norma Shearer, Jean Harlow, Jeanette MacDonald, Myrna Loy, Clark Gable, John Gilbert, Maurice Chevalier, Ricardo Cortez, all three Barrymores, Gary Cooper, Marie Dressler, William Powell, Frank Morgan, Billie Burke, Wallace Berry, Robert Young, Anita Page, and the young hopefuls under contract going to school that no one had heard of yet—Robert Taylor, Mickey Rooney. Muriel Kirkland was from Broadway, as were the Alfred Lunts, Dorothy Burgess, Ina Clare, Rodgers and Hart, Fred Astaire, Dorothy Parker, Anita Loos, Sam Hoffenstein, Sam Behrman, actors, writers, composers, directors, producers, publicists, technicians, Lillian Hellman as script reader, inventors, designers . . . all wanted to come to Hollywood, out of the cold and depression to the land of starlight, star bright, sunshine, fame and money.

The only strange thing about being there was the elusive Twilight Zone quality. It was like quicksilver—if you hold your palm very still, it stays there and shines. But if you try to shut your palm, it disappears. Everything in Hollywood was new and created. It was only a set. No back, no roof, it was all created in a chalk marked square in front of a camera—and you were only as good as your last picture.

I was living in a nice apartment on Sunset Boulevard, up at 5 a.m., shower, breakfast, and out at 5:45. Drive to the studio, arrive 6:30, hairdresser, 6:45 to 7:45. Makeup room next. Put on costume, 8:30—on the set at 8:50. Call to work at 9:00 a.m. ready with all the dialogue to be shot that whole day. Day in, day out the same routine, sometimes to dinner time, repeating every move, every scene, every word until it was covered by long shots, medium and close ups. They were using Pancromatic nitrate film and the kleig lights were murder. The Max Factor greasepaint covered every pore and blemish. It was hot and uncomfortable and wearing it for 12 to 16 hours was enervating and boring.

Things looked promising enough for me to send Irving money to come to Hollywood. I was hopeful that he would finally get a job. I was alone. I can't remember the details of his arrival. All I know is that I realized finally that I had never known him.

In the three years of our marriage we hadn't spent more than three months together. When he arrived, he did not seem particularly interested in my career. After my long hours at the studio and all the cooking and the cleaning afterward, besides learning my lines, I no longer went to the theater in the evenings. We didn't have much chance for communication, and I gave up trying to get him to do anything to help me. He didn't empty an ashtray or wash a dish, and I suppose it was my fault that I didn't demand that he do it. I had no idea what he did when I wasn't around, but when I was, he demanded attention as before, and started to criticize me in a caustic way. My family and friends call me a slow burn because I don't lose my temper. The general opinion is that it is not good to keep harsh feelings bottled up. I don't actually bottle them. I just hate fights and will walk a mile to avoid an argument. It takes me a long time to get mad, but when I do, stay away. It isn't a matter of carrying a grudge; I just cut the people out of my life. I can never be involved with anyone who has insulted my pride or someone for whom I have lost respect.

As I look back at my life, I realize that I have a lot of patience, but very little tolerance for smallness, or lack of courage, or stupidity. My marriage never had a chance.

Irving and I had no emotional contact. I wanted to get out of the house and he wanted a mother. I hated to give up a dream that I would be married once and live happily ever after, but the time had come for me to make a break. I had many new friends in Hollywood from the theater. We met at the studios and had lunch and dinner out, or they gathered at my apartment. They became my comfort and solace. I went from picture to picture in 1933. They were grinding them out like sausages. Without Screen Actors Guild we worked twelve to sixteen hours a day.

I wrote to Mother that I was finally in a big movie. Her letters were lonesome and pathetic. The girls were too young to give her companionship, and without Father she was a lost soul. But she had changed her mind about my career as actress and was now very proud of me. I again became the savior of the family. The little insurance money Father had left would not last long. It was a miracle that with his affliction he had been able to get any insurance.

Rosalie was an awkward teenager, frustrated and unhappy. She had gained a lot of weight. I suggested that Mother send her out to me. When I mentioned it to Irving, he was furious, so I suggested that perhaps it would be a good idea if he went back to New York and tried to get himself a job. I split my bank account with him, and we agreed he would try for six months to see if he could come up with some kind of work. I told him he had to get a job, no matter what. Three months later he was back. He phoned me from an expensive apartment house he had moved into where the rents were at least $400 a month. I was living in one that cost $100. He said there was nothing to do in New York, so he and a friend, who was a writer out of a job, decided to take Hollywood by storm. Since they didn't want to make a wrong impression in a cheap apartment, they took a good one. I asked him what they were using for money. He said, "It's just as easy to be in hock for $400 as it is for $100." That did it. I got rid of my guilt and told him I would file for a divorce.

Taking care of two teenage sisters and a mother were enough

responsibility for me. I paid for the divorce and gave him more of my savings to enable him to buy an interest in a French picture that he could distribute in art theaters in the United States. It was a magnificent film, with Annabella, called *Pol de Carotte*.

He was fortunate that I divorced him because he became fired with ambition to show me that he was capable of a lot more than I gave him credit for. The following year, he married again, a nice girl whose father was a big Buick dealer, and started the first ice arena for ice-skating shows, backed of course by his new father-in-law. The success of that was only marred by his invalid wife, who became a recluse by the time he came back to New York in 1941 to become a Broadway producer. Between 1943 and 1952 he produced *Silk Hat Harry, Sound of Hunting, Clutterback,* and *Bernardine* written by Mary Chase. The night that *Bernardine* opened in New Haven for its first tryout, he dropped dead in his early forties, only a few days after he came to see me, to invite me to the opening of the play.

I felt an emptiness in the pit of my stomach when I heard the news of his death in 1952. It was nineteen years after our friendly divorce was granted for mental cruelty. I remember the ad in the Hollywood *Reporter* announcing that I was free and available. I remember the tearful weekend we spent right after our divorce when he told me how pretty I was, how good I had been to him, and how sorry he was to have bungled it. But it was too late. I saw him off on the train to Denver, Colorado, and I was alone again.

Meanwhile, Rosalie had arrived. She enrolled in school and began making friends. One of her boyfriends, a tall, bright newspaperman, was a frequent caller at our apartment, and I was very fond of him. He was Cecil Brown, a great commentator and newscaster. He was a war correspondent in Rome during the Second World War when William L. Shirer was in Berlin and Edward R. Murrow was in London. Cecil went down on the *Repulse,* and survived, and wrote a great book about his experience in the war. His wife, Martha, and he were later stationed in Tokyo and then in New York, and I have cherished their friendship throughout the years.

Rosalie and I were trying to decide the future for Mother and Lucy in Brooklyn. One day I received a call from Albuquerque. A tearful, little, brave girl of thirteen said, "Barbara, I was afraid you'd say no and I couldn't stand it any longer so I made Mama give me the money to come to California. I'm on a Greyhound bus and will be there tomorrow." I was terrified—my thirteen-year-old kid sister traveling across the country by bus! I thought of what might have happened to her and realized she didn't know me and I didn't really know her. But I couldn't help feeling proud that the Barondess girls had guts.

Lucy arrived—tall, awkward, gangly, but with a beautiful figure, lovely skin, honey-colored hair and gray eyes. At thirteen, she was already taller than I was. She was going to be a beauty. She was thrilled to have a sister who was making a movie with the famous Barrymores. I found myself being a mother whether I wanted it or not. I decided the most important thing I could do for Rosalie (who looked very much like me and sounded like me just enough to be an imitation, not an original) was to get her to lose weight and give her some confidence. I made a bargain with her. If she would reduce to my weight, I would divide my wardrobe fifty-fifty with her. It was a considerable and smashing collection by that time, and I would pay for her ticket back to New York. She worked hard, got the weight down, took the clothes, and went back to our old house in Brooklyn to join Mother. She got a job and became a prize-winning saleswoman. Lucy enrolled in Hollywood High School.

By the time Rosalie arrived back in Brooklyn, Mother decided she wanted to come to California, and I found a bungalow for her and Lucy, while Rosalie stayed at our old house at 1870-55th Street in Brooklyn.

I wanted Mother to create her own life with her own friends and felt she should have Lucy live with her. And so I found myself alone in my apartment and free to do whatever I wanted.

Working in Hollywood at the beginning of the Golden Thirties, as they are now called, was a strange combination of exhilaration and excitement with the industry's tremendous surge. The world outside only existed on the radio and in the newspapers. And the Depression didn't get much front-page space in that Shangri-la.

I was happy about the prospect of working at Paramount and thrilled when Leo got me a boost in salary to $750 a week. Banks were failing, Roosevelt was fighting a losing battle with the Great Depression, but you couldn't tell by me. I was swimming upstream like a salmon. Working at Paramount had another promise for me. Douglas MacLean produced there. I had never looked him up, although he asked me to. Frankly, I thought he wouldn't even remember me. But I hoped that I might run into him. On the second day at the studio, however, I saw him in the commissary and he walked right past me—no recognition—so I decided to give up that idea.

I received another call for a part. This time at Columbia. I hadn't seen Harry Cohn since the first dinner in Hollywood, and I had been warned about his famous "hot seat." When I arrived for my interview and he invited me to the studio executive dining room, I knew I was going to get it. The hot seat was a chair, electronically wired. A young actress would be invited to sit in it, Cohn would press a hidden button at the table, and she would jump up screaming. Mr. Cohn thought that was cute and funny, and many of the girls dissolved into tears from shock and embarrassment. Forewarned and instructed, I bought myself a rubber girdle, so when I sat in the chair nothing happened. Cohn buzzed the button, buzzed again while I looked him straight in the eye. He said, "You must have an ass made of iron." I answered, "No, Mr. Cohn, just rubber." He started to laugh, and so did everybody else at the table. P.S. I got the job! It was a film called *When Strangers Marry* starring Jack Holt. I was happy with the part; it was the second lead; and I found I was working all the time—fifty weeks that first year. That was a tremendous coup for a freelance player. Not one film I was in had been released yet, but I was on my way to independence and able to take care of my family. Mother soon made friends with neighbors, and I didn't see much of her. Lucy loved to hang around the movie studio, making herself useful to me because she loved to see the stars.

At the end of the year *Rasputin* was previewed. At the screening I ran into Douglas MacLean again. His wife, Lorraine, was with him and he introduced her. "I came to see it because I knew you were in it," he said. "Why have you never looked me up?"

I said, "I didn't think you'd remember me."

"I've never forgotten you. I've been following your career since you arrived, and at last we meet again." As I watched the movie, I didn't have a moment of regret or complaint. My heart was full of gratitude, and though I found that my performance had been left mostly on the cutting-room floor, there was enough of me left in the picture to make me feel that I was on my way. I didn't know where but at least I was moving in the right direction. I was in the movies, the most romantic business, at the height of the Depression, making $750 a week, when most Americans couldn't get 40 cents an hour. As the press clippings filled my scrap book, I often wondered if Jed ever saw the publicity and notices in New York. His career was getting erratic and slipping. *The Lake*, with Katharine Hepburn, was shredded by the critics. He was now referred to as paranoic, and though I knew that I would never forget the pain and humility of my experience, I didn't wish him any hard luck. I wondered if maybe God was protecting me and I had to go through the agony to find independence and self-discipline.

Nineteen thirty-four was boiling with activity. The writers, Scott Fitzgerald, Nathanael West, Dashiell Hammett, S. J. Perelman, S. N. Behrman, Sam Hoffenstein, Theodore Dreiser, Anita Loos and Lillian Hellman, who was getting $50.00 per week in the Script Department—all were there with the composers, lyricists, stars and hopefuls. They kept coming in droves to live in the rooming houses and clubs . . . to take abuse and insults from the five horrors that controlled the most glamorous asylum in the world.

CHAPTER THIRTEEN

Love

WHILE MOTHER made new friends, I made my own life. I found that the movie colony was broken up into cliques. If you wanted to be in the Darryl Zanuck set you had to be a star and play croquet. Basil Rathbone and his wife gave the most exclusive and expensive parties in Beverly Hills. There was the George Raft set, the Jack Warner set—they were tennis buffs— the Sam Goldwyn set, and the German contingent, who kept much to themselves but occasionally were at Ernst Lubitsch's parties. The Russians played low profile and stuck together.

Lucy was in high school and hanging around with me in her spare time. I moved to the Chateau De Fleur apartments, a Spanish California version of a French chateau, on Fountain Avenue in Hollywood; but it had an elevator and was modestly fashionable. If you didn't have a house with a swimming pool, this was a dignified place to stay. The management liked me and they let me redecorate my apartment, choose my own colors, draperies and bedspreads. It was attractive and simple.

One day I came in from a luncheon and was looking for my script to start studying my part for a new picture the next day. When I couldn't find it, I was worried. Lucy came home from

school and I asked her if she had seen it. I was being outfitted at
Paramount for *Luxury Liner,* a picture in which I played a bitchy
socialite. The star was Zita Johan, a talented actress from Broadway, who made a hit in *Machinal.* (Opposite her in that play was
a skinny young actor with bad teeth and big ears, not very
impressive. When MGM took him in hand and gave him the
usual going-over, the trimmings, the confidence, the clothes,
and a set of good fitting teeth, he emerged as the superstar Clark
Gable.)

Since Lucy had a key to my apartment, and spent as much
time with me as she did with Mother, I wasn't too surprised to
see her there. She looked frightened. She said: "I'm sorry. I'll get
it back right away. I didn't know you would come home so
early." She had run into Jerry Wald, one of the new recruits, a
columnist on the *Graphic*—he became Walter Winchell's suc-
cessor. He came to Hollywood to make his fame and fortune as a
writer. He was to report to the studio the next day and had never
seen a screenplay. Since I knew Jerry slightly from the Broadway
days, and he knew I was acting in movies, he had asked Lucy for
one of my scripts so he could see how it was set up. I never see
Jerry Wald's name without thinking with a chuckle about the
first script he ever examined, the model for the ghost-writers in
What Makes Sammy Run. He became one of the most successful
producers in the motion picture industry. I found out later that at
that time he had locked up two writers in his apartment to ghost
the first script. They were the twin Epstein boys, Julie and Phil,
who wrote *Three Coins in a Fountain* and many other hits.

Tamara Geva, the dancer, who made a hit on Broadway in
Whoopee and *Three's a Crowd* with Clifton Webb, was then making
films tests at MGM. She brought a handsome young man named
Robert to my apartment who was under stock contract at MGM.
He hadn't been in a picture yet, was waiting for the big break,
and Louis B. Mayer had bought him a dinner jacket. I got to
know him quite well. After Tamara went back to New York to
appear in *Flying Colors* I came home one day with the current
issue of *Movie Magazine* under my arm because it had a picture of

me in it. I found Lucy and Robert washing my car—they wanted to surprise me. I showed them my picture in the magazine. Robert said wistfully, "Barbara, do you think my picture will ever be in a movie magazine?" I looked into a pair of remarkable violet-blue eyes set in a magnificent head. Blue-black hair, perfect teeth, and fair skin—a beautiful masculine face, and I meant it when I said, "I'm sure your picture will not only appear in a magazine but probably on many covers. When you get started there'll be nothing to stop you." To this day Lucy loves to tell how Robert Taylor helped her wash my car.

During those years in Hollywood, we drove or walked through the studio gates in the mornings. We never left until we were completely finished, which was sometimes as late as midnight. We rarely visited anybody else's set, and the commissary was our only meeting place. The superstars and the super heads of the studio we rarely saw, because they had their bungalows and their chefs to cook for them. Only extroverts, like Joan Crawford, would sometimes sail in as she did one day, in a magnificent, black velvet tight-fitting gown, with a red rose in her mouth. It was a crazy and wonderful time. I never saw or was invited to any orgies and I can't believe that all the dirt and gossip that is being dug up by people with large imaginations could have possibly gone on, though I don't doubt excesses were committed behind closed doors. If poor Jean Harlow who died when she was twenty-six years old, for example, had all the affairs that have been credited to her, she would have had to have lived twice as long and would not have had time to work even one day.

I was divorced and getting back into circulation, watching my step carefully. I went to dinner with producers, directors, actors and writers who were willing to be my friends, and I liked being with them. I made it a point never to infringe on a friendship or use it in any way to further my career. I never hesitated to ask a stranger if he had a part for me in a picture, but a friend had to ask me. Maybe it was fear or maybe pride.

I was a free-lancer with a couple of new managers. Douglass

Montgomery was making movies and we resumed our old relationship. I saw a lot of him so I didn't need anyone else. We made a picture together, *Eight Girls in a Boat*, at Paramount. He was good to work with and to be with. The picture was about a girls' school in Switzerland, was made partially on locaton at Arrowhead Lake, and we all had to be there about six weeks. Kay Johnson played the headmistress. Most of the girls were supposed to be from 15 to 18 years old and a lot of them were beauty contest winners playing their first role in movies. Our director, Richard Wallace, and his wife, Mary, a nice, straight-laced couple, felt responsible for the young ladies, and were afraid the electricians and assistant directors and grips would go stir-crazy without their women for six weeks. To keep the young things out of trouble, Dick Wallace insisted on curfew. Everyone had to be in bed by 10 p.m.—lights out—and that meant everybody.

Kay was bored and so were Douglass and I. We were in our twenties and didn't want to be treated like children. So at night when the company was bedded down, the three of us would steal out of our rooms and meet a quarter of a mile away where Douglass had his car. He drove us down the mountains to San Bernardino—a good three quarters of an hour drive—to meet Ramon Navarro and a few chums and party until the wee hours of the morning. This routine took its toll, and after a week I decided the camera couldn't be fooled, and if I kept it up, no one would believe that I was a young teenager. The shadows under my eyes were catching up.

I developed a beautiful defense against the wolves. When I wanted to get rid of a man I would say to him, "You know how we Russians are—so emotional and possessive. If you start anything with me you must be prepared. I might fall madly in love with you, and if I do I'll make a terrible nuisance of myself. So be careful, because I find you terribly attractive." If he was a married man, it was a cinch to stop him. I made it a rule never to go out with a married man. I was sorry for the women who were married to some of those men. They were usually nice, plain girls from small towns who had never dreamed of the kind of success their husbands eventually made in motion pictures. The temptations were so great for these inflated egos, particularly where every girl was a beauty. It's hard to believe, but Ziegfeld could have picked a chorus line from any market, laundry, service station or any other place where girls were employed. It was not even a question of morality with me; it was just a matter of self-esteem.

I was called back to MGM for a part in *Hold Your Man* with Jean Harlow and Clark Gable. Harlow, far from being the tough, dumb, sexy broad that the public knew, was sweet, soft and intelligent. She looked flashy and hard on the screen, but off screen she was a friendly, clear-eyed young woman. Gable, on the other hand, wasn't the most gracious gentleman I had ever met. One day as I was walking to the lot, he caught up with me and with his false teeth flashing, said, "Hey, Barbara, are you blonde all over?" I managed to surpress an urge to tell him off, and simply said, "That depends. But you will never find out."

The producer of *Hold Your Man* was Bernie Hyman. I had met his wife and knew he liked me because he came on the set one day with Jean Harlow's husband (of a few weeks), Paul Bern, who said he had heard good things about me from Bernie. Paul had known Joseph Barondess in New York—the grand old man had died four years before my father. We had a lovely talk about theater versus movies.

I liked Bernie Hyman, and, although he was not an intellectual, I found him to be a gentleman. This was my second role in a picture that he had produced. He had never asked me to go out with him, so I was a little surprised when one afternoon about five, as we were doing our last scene, he came onto the set and asked me what I was doing for dinner. I told him I had an early shooting scheduled for the next morning and was going home to study my script. He said his wife was in Palm Springs and Paul Bern, who was feeling very low, had asked him to dinner. He didn't explain where. I didn't like the idea of going to Paul Bern's house without their wives there. Bernie assured me that we would have dinner at the Ambassador Hotel.

I wasn't afraid of the man; I was just adamant about my reputation. I knew what Louella Parsons could do with an item like that. But Bernie pursuaded me that I would be doing them a favor because Paul was very depressed, and I agreed to go out to dinner if they would make it an early evening and I could leave right afterward. Bernie promised to bring me home early and I went home to remove my make-up and change my clothes.

On the way down, after he picked me up about 7:30, he mentioned that Paul was in a very bad emotional state because of his marriage to Jean. I asked him why—she seemed like a friendly, loving girl. Bernie implied that it was a sexual problem. In those days sex was not discussed at the dinner table as it is today. It wasn't out of style; plenty of it went on but usually behind closed doors. I assumed, from what Bernie said, that Paul's problems were simply a lack of control, because Jean was such a potent sex image that he became impotent. It was humiliating because he was very much in love with her. Bernie told me he was tired of hearing the problem discussed over and over again, for it had become an obsession with Paul. I was sorry for Paul and decided to be lively and entertaining.

When we arrived at the Ambassador, and I saw that we were parking near the private bungalow, I was furious, but I didn't say anything. Paul greeted us at the door. There were only three of us, with a captain and a waiter hovering around, and we had a lovely meal for two and a half hours, with champagne, much general talk, and a little too much drinking, I thought, by Paul Bern. I had a good excuse not to drink more than two glasses of champagne—I simply announced that that was my rule when I was in a picture, and both men respected it.

We left Paul about eleven o'clock. Bernie thanked me for coming along and dropped me at my building.

The shrill ring of the telephone woke me out of a sound sleep. I turned on the light and grabbed the phone. I saw by the clock that it was 4:00 a.m. A man's voice said, "For God's sake, don't mention where you had dinner. Get the morning paper," and hung up. The voice was Bernie's. I couldn't sleep and couldn't imagine what I would find in the newspaper. I was terrified, so I dressed, had several cups of coffee, and went down to an all-night newsstand to see what I could learn. The headlines screamed: "Paul Bern Commits Suicide" and under it in large type was: "Who were the couple that had dinner with him and were the last to see him alive?"

I needed this notoriety like a hole in the head. At the studio I kept my mouth shut. Bernie avoided me and smiled sickly when we did see each other on the lot. The only person who knew about this was Howard Strickland, the head publicist at MGM. I found that out when he said to me one day, months later, "Barbara, you are a lady. Any other girl in your position would have used the dinner at the Ambassador to blackmail the producer into a leading part." I replied, "Howard, that's not the way I operate."

For me this was a narrow escape—I vowed that I would remember this valuable lesson and never again go out with a married man alone. Neither Howard Strickland nor Bernie nor I ever came forward to tell about that dinner with Paul. The papers never identified the mysterious couple. Several books have been written about Harlow, with speculations about Paul. Even Ben Hecht in a newspaper article represented that he knew the truth, but he was wrong. This has been the best-kept secret in Hollywood.

I hadn't been in Hollywood long before I discovered that it was filled with three fears. Number one, the fear that you won't get there; number two, the fear that you won't stay there; and number three, that if you do slip you'll never get back. And that went for extras to the heads of the largest studios, because the powers behind them were the banks, and everyone was like a small ball in a roulette wheel.

Ugly rumors were coming in from Europe; the name Hitler was heard more and more. There was an influx of German and

Austrian talent, and hopefuls from almost all the countries in Europe wanted to catch the ring called Hollywood Star. We had our own problems in America, and the movie industry didn't escape them completely. The Screenwriters Guild and the Screen Actors Guild were formed. The actors were tired of working 16 to 20 hours a day, sometimes without consideration.

I became a member of the Screen Actors Guild. But they were planning a strike, and I was petrified. If the studios did not give in, there was a very good chance that all charter members would be blacklisted and their careers ruined. But the desire to belong somewhere and be a part of something was so strong that it outweighed my fear. My salary was now $1,000 a week—an unbelievable sum in the middle of the Depression for a supporting player who was possibly on her way to becoming rich and famous. Luckily, L. B. Mayer agreed to the terms, the studios signed the contracts and the strike was avoided.

Montgomery was back in my life. We assumed our rare camaraderie and mutual respect. There was no emotional attachment; neither of us were possessive. Whenever we picked up, it was as if we had seen each other just the day before, and it went on that way between marriages and romances, both his and mine.

My friend Lou Alter married again. At his house I met Theodore Drieser for the second time. Among the men I went out with were Arthur Hornblow, producer, a little more intellectual than the run of the mill, and a couple of times Freddie Brisson, whose father, Carl, was under contract at Paramount. I was invited to parties at Ernst Lubitsch's and Larry Hart's, where one was sure to see Richard Rodgers, Herbie Fields, Edgar Selwyn, Ona Munson, Dorothy Parker, Johnnie Green, and almost everyone under contract with MGM. Most of them seemed to be forever waiting for an assignment and all were terribly frustrated. Some of them sat in their offices without ever being called for months. Richard Rodgers, Larry Hart and Herbert Fields wrote a Broadway musical, *I Married an Angel*, on MGM time. Sam Hoffenstein, the poet, and my old friend S. N. Behrman were fortunate enough to get an assignment on a Garbo picture.

It seemed to me that 90 percent of Broadway came and went between 1930 and 1936. Some just got paid and did nothing. The majority hated Hollywood but needed the money. Dorothy Parker got bored sitting in her office; no one came to see her for weeks. She put a sign on her door that read "Gentlemen." Believe me, she got some visitors!

Most of the producers had very little education, a lot of shrewdness, tremendous nerve, and a minimum of intellect. Most of them were gross and unattractive. They found themselves in a business they had never dreamed of in the silent days. There were few with the talent of Charles Chaplin. He was one of a kind, and he alone controlled his output. People were thrilled to climb onto the bandwagon called Hollywood. A very few made it to stardom, fame and fortune. Egos could become inflated like balloons, then collapse with a prick of a pin and be discarded. I know of very few in the movies who were in complete control of their careers. There are exceptions and you can count them on one hand. Even the giant producer of the top studio, "Mr. God, L. B. Mayer," was eventually removed by the banks. What the movies needed—besides beautifully run and trained teams of technical talent: camera men, soundmen, script girls, and makeup people, who took up the first nine rows at a preview—were some people with brains and character instead of gross egotistical Heads of Studios. If they had had that, the results might not have been so hit and miss.

The competition among the studios was fascinating. MGM had Garbo; her pictures didn't make money but she had quality and class. Paramount had Dietrich; Warners had Bette Davis. Sam Goldwyn wanted someone like that, so he imported a fine Russian actress, Anna Sten. She photographed like a dream and they spent a million dollars promoting her. But she came through on the screen like a carbon copy and her career was over in a flash. She lacked that intangible charisma that makes contact with the audience.

Lorraine and Douglas MacLean added me to their circle. When she had a date with the attractive Richard Halliday, who

was based at Paramount's in New York and was her then current
crush (long before he married Mary Martin), she or Douglas
decided that I was perfect for a foursome. After a few weeks on
Douglas's yacht, *The Comrade*, and in Palm Springs, I wondered
about this cozy arrangement. He was a married man treating his
wife as if she were his sister and being most attentive to me. I
found this design for living flattering, interesting and uncomfortable. Douglas was a handsome, elegant gentleman, once an
important silent movie star and now one of the top comedy
producers in Hollywood. Douglas's family and background had
nothing to do with the theater, but when Douglas, at the age of
18, met Daniel Frohman at a dinner party, Frohman said,
"Young man, you should become an actor. We need gentlemen
who can speak the King's English in the American theater."
Frohman later introduced Douglas to Anita Loos and her husband, John Emerson, who both recommended that Douglas go
to the American Academy in New York City. Douglas enrolled
there and did well. On graduation night, a performance was
given by the graduating class as usual—it was always seen by
many Broadway actors and producers. On this night Maude
Adams was present and was so charmed by Douglas's performance that she made the unprecedented gesture of asking him to
take a part with her on Broadway in a curtain raiser by James
Barrie, *The Legend of Lenora*.

After that, Douglas went on to play a lead opposite Alice
Brady, was chosen by Mary Pickford to play opposite her in
Captain Kidd Junior in 1917 and went into the movies, where he
produced movies independently and played in them. He appeared in *Soft Cushions*, his only talkie. Paradoxically, he, with
his fine voice, stopped acting about the time the movies began to
talk. Before that he acted in nineteen pictures between 1918–29,
wrote four, and produced twenty for RKO and Paramount. He
brought Wheeler and Woolsey, Edna Mae Oliver, Charlie Ruggles and Mary Boland to the screen. He produced and wrote *Six
of a Kind* with Burns and Allen, Ruggles and Boland, and W. C.
Fields and Alison Skipworth. In another film, *Ladies Should Lis-*

ten, he suggested to Cary Grant that he play roles for comedy rather than straight. He also produced *So Red the Rose* with Margaret Sullavan and *Mrs. Wiggs of the Cabbage Patch* with Pauline Lord.

Douglas was sixth generation American, with a family tree that went back to the Scottish MacLean and Douglas clans. He was proud of his ancestry. He was the only one of his family who didn't follow a navy career. His sister was married to Admiral Mayo's son and they had planned a navy career for him. He had been slated for Annapolis. I was proud that he wanted me. I can't say that I was very happy about the fact that he was married, and I was in a situation that I never dreamed I'd be a part of. A few years before maybe I would not have consented to, or slipped into it, but with Father dead, Mother remarried, and Rosalie engaged, it was my life now, and I wanted him at any cost. I was impressed and wondered what part they wanted me to play in this combination. No one gave me a clue. I decided to watch and listen.

Douglass Montgomery asked me to go to San Francisco with him by boat on an overnight ride. We went off and had a ball. A day or two afterward, the MacLeans said they had tried to reach me and were curious as to where I had been. I decided it was none of their business.

A couple of weeks later Douglass Montgomery, Tommy Wanamaker of the illustrious Wanamaker family in Philadelphia, and Judith Anderson decided that a trip to Mexico would be fun, and we disappeared for another weekend. Montgomery, Tommy and Judith left the driving to me—I couldn't and wouldn't consume the amount of liquor they drank. They stopped urging me and decided that I would be useful as a chauffeur. It was Tommy's car, a foreign make and new to me, but by now I was a good and careful driver, and had a lot of respect for other people's possessions. How we got across the border at Tijuana, I don't know; we didn't have any passports. My three companions drank out of a flask on the way and by the time we got to the border they were smashed.

We checked into a hotel with a string of connecting rooms and proceeded to paint the town red. The two days we spent were a kaleidoscope of bars, restaurants, shopping, and a brothel they insisted on going to, because it had a peep show. I never saw a woman drink as much as Judith did that weekend and still stay on her feet. I remember shopping because I ended up with a bottle of perfume Montgomery bought for me, and when they took me to the brothel peep show, I wanted to throw up. It was about three a.m. of the second night. I told Douglass I had to go to the bathroom and sneaked out to the car to lie down on the backseat to renew my strength and energy. This kind of a drinking contest weekend was not my idea of fun and frolic. I tried to get comfortable in the backseat and lie down, but my head was reeling. I was aware that even drinking one-fourth of the amount they were consuming was too much for me. I was playing with fire. This on-again off-again affair with Montgomery was getting a little too casual—it was an escape for me. I had wanted to liberate myself from the provincial belief that sex and love had to be synonymous with marriage. Everyone around me was leading a liberated, free-wheeling life. I had to get over being a square. Practicing with Montgomery was perfect when it was private. But this foursome went against the grain. Even the connecting rooms in the hotel were embarrassing. I wondered how we were registered, and shuddered at the thought of the hotel register record. I felt uneasy and didn't like it, and I couldn't get MacLean out of my mind. And I wondered what he would think about this drunken weekend.

This was the second time in my life I had been to a brothel. The first time was in Paris. I found the idea revolting. I knew kinky sex existed, but I didn't know anyone who was interested or even talked about it. Strangers' bodies and private parts don't interest me, and I don't have a desire to see people behave like animals in heat. I walked around, shook my head to get it clear, and finally dozed off for what seemed like seconds. I woke at the sound of their voices, the dawn was breaking and I drove them back to the hotel, where they fell into a dead sleep. By the time they woke up with terrible hangovers, I had been out for a couple of hours, had breakfast, and revived sufficiently to tackle the trip back to Beverly Hills. When I was questioned by the MacLeans again, because they had called me to go yachting, this time I told them where I had been. Lorraine expressed her admiration of Douglass Montgomery, and I promised to introduce them.

My work continued steadily. I played the part of an Austrian duchess in an RKO picture, *The Fountain,* with Ann Harding, Brian Aherne and Paul Lucas. Then a couple of independents, another picture at Columbia, *When Strangers Marry,* in which I played a heavy second lead, and a picture called *Collision* with Eddie Arnold, in which I was a sexy hooker. My salary was raised. I should have been happy, and I was in the money, but I thought the parts were trivial and stupid. Most of the time 90 percent of my scenes were cut.

Walter Wanger was producing *Queen Christina* at MGM. Rouben Mamoulian, the great director of the Theatre Guild in New York, was having a romance with Garbo and directing her in this one. When they called me to play the part of a sexy, funny maid at the inn, at first I refused. Mamoulian told me that although the part was short, it was important because the scene was with Garbo and John Gilbert and had to be played expertly. He also said they would be willing to pay me quite a bit of money. I told my agent; he negotiated; and the Hollywood *Reporter* announced, "BARONDESS SIGNED WITH GARBO." I was paid $9,000 for that bit and saw my opportunity to win my bet with Walter Winchell and get national publicity. All went as planned. Winchell paid me $500, and I was delighted when he announced on his Sunday program that I had won the bet. The only thing my agent forgot was to be sure I received a screen credit.

I wrote a short article headed "I Act With Garbo" and sold it to a movie magazine. Garbo and Walter were mad at me for a month, and then all was forgiven, and I was engaged to play in *A Tale of Two Cities* with Ronald Colman, Isabel Jewell, and Blanche Yurka as a leader in the French Revolution. Mine was a juicy part that took a month to film. It was a David O. Selznick Production. I had a beautiful death scene in which I jumped for a drawbridge that was pulled up as I fell in the gully below. This was an opportunity every actress dreams of—to play a death scene in a sympathetic role. The director decided that it was too dangerous for me to grab the end of the bridge and stand there as they drew it up, so they dressed a small stunt man in a costume exactly like mine, made him up, and put a wig on him to look like me as much as possible in this long shot. When my mother saw the picture, after telling all her neighbors that her beautiful daughter was in it, she called me, horrified. All she saw was a flash of the double falling from the bridge. Because she was looking for me, she saw something that no one in a million would notice in a scene with so many people: my double had hairy arms. I convinced her that the only thing left of me in the film was one flash leading the revolution and that the falling figure was a double. The whole part ended up on the cutting room floor.

So *A Tale of Two Cities* was another terrible disappointment to me. My dream of building a solid career didn't look very promising. On the other hand, in the midst of a depression when people were starving, my salary kept going up. I was still swimming upstream like a salmon. The producers, writers and directors were just as frightened as everyone else; they had no more control over their careers than the actors, and their success too depended on how good their last picture was. They were all in a fierce race, and they had no consideration or mercy. The new Screen Actors Guild gave us a little protection. The bosses could never again work actors until they dropped from exhaustion, sometimes twenty hours without a stop.

I realized Hollywood was pretty good to me. I was getting my chance for a career, and an opportunity to catch the ring of fame and maybe love; but it wasn't happening fast enough, and I had a constant feeling of expectancy. Irving Thalberg died. I never met the man who was responsible for my being in Hollywood. Hitler and Mussolini were devastating Europe and Africa. Pro-

fessional actors on Broadway were working in the Federal Theatre Project for a maximum salary of $103.40 a month. I felt a
little guilty about the ridiculous amount of money that I was
making for the lousy parts I was playing, but one can always find
an excuse to become an ostrich, and as much as I wanted to be
noble and think about what was going on in the world, I stayed
in my self-centered life.

Douglass Montgomery asked me to fly to New York for the
Mayfair Ball, held for the elite of Broadway every Saturday night
at the Ritz. We made a date to meet under the lamppost at
Sutton Place, corner of 56th Street—our romantic spot—go to
the ball on Saturday, and fly back on Sunday. It sounds pretty
extravagant when you think it took twenty-four hours to fly to
New York, with two stops for refueling in Kansas City and
Chicago. But we did some crazy things in those days to release
the tension.

Montgomery stayed on because he was offered a play. I flew
back because I was scheduled for *The Merry Widow,* with Maurice
Chevalier and Jeanette MacDonald, directed by Ernst Lubitsch. I
was to play the chief coquette at Maxim's with whom Prince
Danillo had a little flirtation. To distinguish me from the other
coquettes whose costumes were pastel (and came out shades of
grey in the movie), Adrian designed a smashing black one for
me. It must have caught Chevalier's eye, because he asked me to
have dinner with him. What could be more exciting? As a date,
Chevalier was a self-centered dud. On the whole the picture was
a happy experience; the atmosphere was one of song and dance,
and Lubitsch was a pleasure to work for.

My sister Lucy got into the act, so to speak. She hung around
the set pretending to be my personal maid, because she was
fascinated with the Albertina Rasch dancers. When Tamara Geva
came to visit me one day she saw Lucy imitating the dancers at
the side of the stage. Tamara encouraged her and said she would
speak to her former husband, George Balanchine, and try to get
her a scholarship at the American School of Ballet, which she
did.

As soon as we got the news I made plans to take Lucy back to New York to enroll her in school and live with Rosalie, who had married the boy next door in Brooklyn. Lucy was almost fifteen years old. I made arrangements to take the train to New York and mentioned it to the MacLeans two weeks before going. Douglas told me that by coincidence he and Lorraine were planning a trip to New York, so we might be there the same time. He asked me what hotel I intended to stay in and I told him the Algonquin. I was busy with preparations and did not talk to them again before Lucy and I boarded the train. It was my first ride back since my arrival a little over two years before (not counting the crazy weekend flight). Sitting on the train I thought about Baron, the car I still had, the eight or ten pictures I had already made. As Lucy and I were reminiscing, she said, "This is different from my ride in the Greyhound bus." There was a knock at the door. I said, "Come in," and there was Douglas MacLean, debonair, with a grin on his face. "Surprise!" he said.

It didn't take long to find out that Lorraine had left the week before and was having a fling around New York with Richard Halliday. On the train Douglas indicated that he and Lorraine had an amicable agreement to go their own ways. He was sixteen years older than Lorraine and twenty-one years older that I—a magnificent man in his prime. I saw that his ego was hurt, but that he was putting up a smiling, sophisticated front. He had not been married to Lorraine long, a few years. She was a fun-loving, stunning woman, very much the Irene Dunne type. All I knew about her was that her name had been Lorraine Kelly. Lucy found someone her age to talk to in the Club Car, and this was our first time to be alone. He told me that he was attracted to me and thought I was beautiful and brilliant, a fine actress, and all the things I liked to hear. But he didn't mention divorce and I was disturbed by his ardent declarations. I was very attracted to him and didn't like it. "Here I go again," I thought. We had dinner and spent hours together, with Lucy present. Everything about him, his looks, beautiful teeth and hands—his natural grace, voice, manners and elegance—appealed to me. I realized that I liked this man very much and I was afraid this meant trouble.

The Paramount publicity department was meeting Douglas at the train at Grand Central, and the MGM publicity department was meeting me. Before we said our goodbyes, he asked if I would join him and Lorraine for dinner that night. They were staying at the Pierre. I told him I already had a date with a New York friend. He asked me to please bring him along. I told him I would have to let him know. I had a busy morning. After checking in at the Algonquin I had lunch with Rosalie and her husband and they took Lucy with them to Brooklyn. I was to remain in New York for two weeks. When I came back to the hotel, I found a bouquet of three dozen talisman roses with the following note:

> I climbed a dark unfriendly stair
> To find a welcome waiting there
> And a smile that put to rout
> The shadows round about.
>
> Of course the shadows really stayed
> But I'm sure they were dismayed
> To join an accidental meeting
> That proffered such a happy greeting.
>
> There was I and there were you
> Then was nineteen thirty-two.

signed "Because you're wonderful. Douglas."

I was touched and stunned. This man had the pick of anybody in Hollywood. There were few of his quality in the movie business. He was obviously a prince and a prize. I didn't believe there was a chance of our getting together. I considered him as unattainable as the President of the United States. Obviously if I was willing to take it on as an affair, it was a cinch. But did I want that with him? I have never thought of myself as a subject for

Back Street. This was a difficult decision to make, because I didn't want to lose him.

My date reluctantly agreed to join the MacLeans for dinner and we went to the Rainbow Room. My date was an attractive man who had flown out to California to see me and was getting to the point of asking me to marry him. When he saw Douglas romancing me on the dance floor, he got the message and I never heard from him again.

The two weeks in New York were heady for me. I guess they were for all of us. We went in a foursome to the theater and opera, dining and dancing every night. There was always a date for Lorraine—not always Richard Halliday. And at least two or three times a week I had lunch or cocktails with Douglas. The second day he insisted on my meeting him at the Playhouse Theatre in front of William Brady's office, where we had met the first time, and that's where he kissed me for the first time. His words were carefully chosen, his voice seemed sheer poetry, everything about him seemed impeccable and immaculate. He knew how to romance a girl! I had never met anyone like him. After lunch, he suggested the Metropolitan Museum. I told him it had been my favorite place when I was hunting for a job in the theater. He told me that the American Wing was his favorite. He opened my eyes to the beauty of good American furniture. And in so doing, he opened the door for me to something I had never thought about. He had grown up in Philadelphia and was a collector of antiques: he loved and appreciated them.

We went to the Casino in the Park for cocktails. Before we parted, to meet later for Noel Coward's *Conversation Piece*, we stopped at a bookstore and he bought me the first book I ever owned about antiques.

The days flew. We saw *Accent on Youth* by Sam Raphaelson, a play about a young girl in love with a middle-aged writer. Douglas said it was a perfect part for me to do on the screen. He said he would like to buy the play and produce it. He was sure that this part would pave the way for my becoming a star.

Beautiful promises; everything was suddenly too frightening
and too perfect.

The day after cocktails in the park I received another poem:

Evening.
　　Cocktails in the park.
　　Twilight shadows
　　Melt into the dark.

　　Whispers.
　　Soft and dim the lighting.
　　Hands across the table,
　　Eager lips inviting.

　　Taxi
　　Whirling down to Forty-Four.
　　Wanting more,
　　Sigh and leave you at your door.

That evening Douglas announced that he had to go back to
Hollywood on October 26. Lorraine, who was going to remain
for another ten days, tried to persuade me to go back with
Douglas to keep him company. But I was determined to stay in
New York as long as she did. Douglas bought a present for
Lorraine and a duplicate for me—a beautiful enamel evening
bag, one for her in white and one for me in black. I told him I
had to stay because I had an interview with Sam Harris about a
play, and that was perfectly true—an opportunity to take the
leading part in a play for Sam Harris would be the perfect move
for me. And I was afraid to face Douglas in Hollywood for ten
days alone.

Just before leaving California I had rented a tiny house on
Hollywood Boulevard, with a white picket fence, unfurnished
and I was looking forward to going back to my first house and
furnishing it. Douglas left as scheduled on October 26. I received
a wire from the train on October 27: "Awfully, Douglas." I de-

cided that I had better have a talk with Lorraine. We made a date at Sardi's. October 28, "Lonesome, Douglas." October 29: "Have been wishing today that your interview would be all you could hope for. Tonight's sunset is quite as colorful as those we shared, just as much green but there's a lot of lonesomeness in it. Douglas."

I met Lorraine at Sardi's and got a corner table at the back where we could talk privately. Lorraine was amusing, witty, her usual scintillating self. The luncheon was full of "girl talk." I felt nervous and didn't know how to bring up the subject. When we got to our fourth cup of coffee, I couldn't stand it any longer, and I blurted out, "Lorraine, I don't know what your arrangement is with Douglas, but you are encouraging his flirtation with me!" She looked at me with surprise and said, "Don't be silly, Barbara, we are both very fond of you."

"It's all very well for you to say that," I replied, "but you are playing with fire. I don't know what I feel for Douglas at this moment and I have no idea how he feels about me, but this is a very ticklish situation. Douglas has all the qualities I've always admired in a man. I'm very attracted to him, so I want to go on record to tell you that if I should fall in love with him, I would fight for him. It's up to you."

"Barbara, don't be so Russian and dramatic. Douglas loves me and I love him. We have worked out a way of life that suits us perfectly. We keep our individualities and have our freedom. We have no intention of ever getting a divorce. So have your fun, now that you've warned me, and relax. The subject is closed."

I went back to my hotel where I found another wire: "What is happening? Where are you? What plans? Awfully, Douglas."

I didn't answer, but made up my mind to go back to California. When my train arrived in Chicago, I was handed this wire by the station master: "My spies inform me, why not you? And my wire unanswered. Why the frost? It is still spring here. Should I be happy or sad tell me. Douglas." I answered. The next communique read: "Happy, excited, thrilled, joyous, and awfully makes exactly ten words. Douglas." The following read: "Will Thursday ever come. What is your new Los Angeles address? Must know for special reasons. Perhaps we can meet for lunch anyway not later than cocktail hour from then on. Please telephone soon after arrival. Awfully, Douglas."

The special reason was my new little house filled with flowers. The roses, talisman—I had never seen so many in one place. We had cocktails and dinner. I didn't tell him about my conversation with Lorraine. She arrived the following morning and immediately called to invite me to join them for a weekend on the yacht. And that's the way it went for six months. We were a constant foursome; I was treated like one of the family and was never left out of any of their plans. I felt hypnotized and was falling in love. For her it was the perfect case of having her cake and eating it too. Every time he bought her a diamond bangle for her bracelet, he bought three gold ones for me. The subjects were always symbolic but not identical; he bought me a little gold replica of the Twentieth Century train, a telephone with a dial that read "Hello" and "I Love You," and two gold and white enameled cigarettes to commemorate our favorite song, "Two Cigarettes in the Dark." I was mesmerized by the scene, and couldn't walk away from it.

Lorraine decided that she wanted to act. Douglass Montgomery was back in town to do a play and she went to see if she could get into it. She told Montgomery that she was a friend of mine, and asked him to join us for dinner. When he heard that I was going to be there he accepted, and the four of us spent a very strained evening. The next day Montgomery said, "Wow! You can certainly get yourself into situations." And I answered, "What can I do? I am Russian and romantic." He was a good two-fisted drinker, and so was Lorraine. Douglas, however, was a very erratic drinker—on our trip to New York everybody ran to a bar between the acts of a play. Six or eight drinks a night were the norm for Lorraine and most of her cronies. I never saw MacLean or Montgomery drunk . . . but Lorraine was another story. I could never forget Frank and Alma Morgan's bouts with alcohol on that memorable tour of the U. S. in *Topaze*. That gave me an ever-present fear of making a fool of myself.

CHAPTER FOURTEEN

My First Home

THE SITUATION I had gotten myself into became more complicated when Douglas told me he had actually bought the
rights to *Accent on Youth*. He planned to tell Ernst Lubitsch, then
acting head of production at Paramount, that he wanted me for
the leading role. I was both flattered and apprehensive about
this. After he saw Lubitsch, Douglas came to me enraged and
told me that Lubitsch had said: "Douglas, we have Sylvia Sidney
under contract. She's already got a name and is perfect for the
part." Douglas responded that parts *make* actors. As for the
name, he said, "We have Herbert Marshall for the man. I've
bought this play for Barbara, and I'm going to fight to have her
play in it."

I was flabbergasted. This had never happened to me before.
No one had ever fought for me, and this was unsettling—I had
trouble sorting out my feelings. This was the opportunity I'd
worked for and dreamed about. I was in love with a wonderful
man who encouraged me and was giving me the chance to
stretch my talents and potential. Why was I doubting my good
fortune? Something told me to look at it objectively. Maybe my
ambition was bigger than my talent. Douglas was trying to let

me know in every way how important I was to him. Should I let him fight for me, or would it be easier for both of us if I bowed out in favor of Sylvia Sydney? An inner voice reminded me that everyone in Hollywood knew that he and I were good friends and more. It was inevitable that eyebrows would be raised and you'd hear the familiar crack, "The best way to get ahead in Hollywood is to get under a good producer and work up." Did I want a chance at stardom at this price? I was twenty-eight years old, had been acting for nine years, and had had one disappointing love affair and one lousy marriage. Was this the kind of opportunity I had worked for all these years?

Another voice asked whether, after all, at this point I really wanted a career as a leading woman. I don't know if it was rationalization or fear, but I told myself that as a character actress I could go on making a good living for a long time. I could even go back to the stage with a better-known name. I would be over thirty when the picture was released. Did I want a chance of a full personal life with Douglas, or did I want that fleeting, unsatisfactory, debilitating excitement of stardom?

Somehow, much of the movie business seemed tarnished. From the first stories I had heard about Harry Cohn and starlets and the "hot seat," to the tragedy of Paul Bern's suicide, I had come to understand and to know the fear, hate and insecurity surrounding most of the big names. And the grossness behind the expensive glitter! I thought of the day that Gary Cooper— one of the few screen stars that I admired—came up behind me as I walked to a set dressed as a nun, and gave me an old-fashioned pinch on the bottom. It was both hilarious and unsettling—like so much of movie land.

Douglas didn't press me for a decision, but I hated to keep juggling these thoughts without coming to a decision. If I turned down the chance, I might regret it for the rest of my life. If I let Douglas talk Lubitsch into taking me on, and if the movie flopped, Douglas's opinion of me might be shattered.

I came to realize that the important thing in my life was Douglas—more so than a potential career as a star. I loved my independence, but I also had a tremendous need for Douglas—his wisdom, experience, warmth and encouragement. That was the main thing—yes, I could say that without hesitation. I loved this man completely without reservation. In his arms I melted into a state of bliss. He was tender and thoughtful. We clung together. I loved his slim, elegant body, his sensitive hands, his beautiful teeth and his magnificent cultured voice. Everything about him gave me pleasure and I was so proud that he loved me.

I told him that I didn't want the responsibility of the part. When I said that he was more important to me than the inevitably short career I might have, he said that his admiration for me had been multiplied by a hundred. "It takes courage to make a decision like that, darling. I don't know if you are the smartest or dumbest girl I've ever met," he added. I suspect he may have felt relief as well as love. He was not a fighter.

My career as a supporting actress kept going along nicely. One of the best parts offered me about this time by Arthur Hornblow was *Pursuit of Happiness*, written by Lawrence Langer. It was a funny second lead, introduced on Broadway by a good comedienne, Denie More, and had a good cast—Joan Bennett, Charlie Ruggles, Mary Boland, Francis Lederer. I was making $1,500 a week, and had my nice little house that belonged to Decla Dunning's mother. I had my books and a few personal drawings and pictures. It was friendly and homey.

Rosalie and Lucy were unhappy about Mother's choice of the man she wanted to marry. They thought him very inferior to Father. I agreed that he was pretty ordinary, but had to point out that if she was happy with him, that was more important than anything else. Since they were not willing to live with her, they had no right to choose her husband, and she was too young to give up male companionship for the rest of her life. I told them to stop criticizing and give her their blessing.

Mother decided to sell the house in Brooklyn and Rosalie and Lucy decided to live there until it was sold. Rosalie's husband, Bernard Conove, was going to college, and she started her career as a super salesperson on her own. Lucy was enrolled in the Balanchine School of Ballet, but at fifteen was too old to start that rigorous regimen, so after a year, she left the school and married Cecil Joseph at sixteen. She got herself a job at Bergdorf Goodman modeling. She had grown into a beauty. Both of the girls were independent, and I felt free of responsibility for the first time in years.

Montgomery was back in town and we became a famous foursome again. Two Douglasses! When Lorraine and I talked about our Douglasses, nobody knew which belonged to whom and it got to be a running gag—your Douglas, my Douglass or our Douglasses. Strange that as different as she and I were in looks and personality, we seemed to like the same men.

It wasn't long before the foursome broke up again: she and Montgomery went one way, and MacLean and I another. Their drinking increased, and ours decreased. I was happy when MacLean decided to cut out hard liquor and we switched to wine, and not very much of that either. He blamed himself for the breakup of his marriage, and was becoming melancholy about living under the same roof as Lorraine but not seeing much of her. He was also becoming more and more unhappy about his career at Paramount. He and Lubitsch didn't hit it off.

Douglas and I spent a lot of weekends alone on his beautiful yacht, *The Comrade*, and the inevitable finally happened. We became lovers. When I asked Douglas if his mother might be upset with my Jewish background, he looked at me quizzically and said, "I never heard her express any objection to Jesus' background."

He was the most considerate, tender, understanding, amusing and satisfactory man I had ever known. He knew my background—my lack of formal education and religious upbringing, my father's spiritual guidance. I kept nothing from him. He told me about his family, members of the MacLean Clothier family of Philadelphia. He introduced me to his mother, who was almost eighty-six years old and living in Los Angeles. He had been a change-of-life baby. She was a remarkable, alert, sweet woman, interested in everything and everybody around her. She told me about his father, a dedicated and famous Methodist clergyman who was sent to a different city every three years to put an ailing church on its feet; about his sisters, one dead, the other Aida, living in Philadelphia, married to Admiral Mayo's son, Captain Chester Mayo of the Navy. I heard fascinating tales about Admiral Mayo's role in our taking over the Panama Canal. I was given a picture of Douglas's father at the age of six, standing on a platform with Abraham Lincoln at his nomination acceptance speech in Philadelphia, with four of his uncles and grandfather on the platform behind Lincoln—taken by Mathew Brady.

Douglas and Lorraine were divorced on March 17, 1936, St. Patrick's Day. Douglas said that was the day the snakes were driven out of Ireland. The news made me very happy. Married to me or not, he seemed more mine. Since he had no offers from any major studios, he found himself without work for the first time in his life. It was a difficult period for him. An independent studio suggested that he remake a picture that had made him a star as a young man in the silent days when he was leading man to Mary Pickford. The picture was *Twenty Three and a Half Hours' Leave*. He was determined to find an unknown young actor and give him a chance at stardom.

We spent a lot of time on *The Comrade* with a few close friends, and I became chief cook and bottlewasher. After he made his settlement with Lorriane, he mentioned money for the first time. I gathered that he owned important real estate, had some investments, but not much cash. His and Lorraine's clique of friends disappeared. They were convinced I was a fortune hunter. I suggested that he rent his house on North Linden because he spent so little time in it. He was with me every night at my house, and we were on *The Comrade* weekends. He agreed it was a good idea, immediately rented it to Rosalind Russell, and took an apartment.

Naturally, I thought a great deal about our possible marriage but kept it to myself. I was afraid that our backgrounds were too dissimilar. He, on the other hand, talked gloomily about his failure as a husband, and I knew, although he didn't admit it, that he was depressed about his career. He did make *Great Guy* with James Cagney and *Twenty Three and a Half Hours' Leave,* and another film, *The Life of Franz Schubert* with Ilona Massey, a beautiful Hungarian actress with a lovely singing voice. None were hits. Without the backup of big studio distribution and publicity, he found it a tough battle to get a picture released, and he was sorely disappointed.

He had been divorced several months when we were invited by old friends of his, Doris and Hal Cooley, to spend the weekend in Laguna. The Cooleys kept urging us to get married. I refused to get into the conversation. I was petrified, but they kept it up. Suddenly, Douglas looked at me and said, "Come on, sweetheart, Mexico is only a couple of hours away." He turned to our hosts and said, "Let's go."

The four of us drove to Laredo, Mexico, just across the border. It was a dingy, ugly little town, plastered with signs advertising easy marriages and divorces. We walked into the dirty old courthouse. Hal talked to some man in a shiny suit who got us the license that was necessary. Doris and Hal were our witnesses and without ceremony or conversation, the marriage was performed by a Mexican judge. I became Mrs. Douglas MacLean.

Somehow, it never seemed real in a foreign language. All Douglas and I had to do was sign our names on a piece of paper that I never saw again. I was in a slight daze because he hadn't even asked me, just told me to come along. There was no question that this was what I wanted, but I hadn't even heard the familiar words of the marriage ceremony. I said, "Darling, what happened to love, honor and obey? Until death do us part?" He grinned and replied, "I have always questioned the validity of 'till death do us part,' because if no man should put asunder what God has put together, how could we both have been divorced?" I decided that I had married the most intelligent man in the world, and all I wanted to do was to please him and hear him laugh.

My little house had two bedrooms and two baths. He moved

in with me. I was Mrs. Douglas MacLean. He started to plan a long honeymoon trip, because for the first time in many years he had no plans to hold him down. He wanted to go someplace glorious and new. We talked about many places and decided on the Orient. In those days the trip took two months coming and going, so we planned a five- or six-month voyage. He laid down certain rules because, he insisted, what is wrong with most marriages is too much familiarity. To keep the glamour and precious excitement that we had in our relationship, he insisted that we never share a bedroom or bathroom. He said he would always treat me like a date; by preserving our privacy we would preserve our marriage. It didn't take me long to see that he was right. He never saw me unless I was ready to be seen, and I never saw him sloppy, unshaven or unattractive, unless, of course, one of us was ill. I always had my romantic leading man.

There were only two lines traveling at that time to the Orient, one Canadian and one Japanese. We left on the Japanese *Tatsuta-Maru*. The trip from Los Angeles to Honolulu took about five days. We stayed in Waikiki one evening, long enough to feel the glorious velvet air and see the magnificent flowers and smell the pungent aroma of the tuberoses and gardenias. We left early the next morning for Yokohama, twenty-one days.

We made friends with our fellow passengers, especially one couple from England, Sigmund Gestetner and his wife Hennie, a Swiss girl. They were on their honeymoon too. His family were the famous multigraph machine inventors and manufacturers before the birth of Xerox. According to Douglas's plan, we had two staterooms. Every night he made a date to meet me for cocktails. He never knew what I was going to wear or how I was going to look until we met in the lounge. It was a game we kept up through our marriage. I loved every minute. I counted my blessings in having a handsome, thoughtful, exciting husband, whom I revered, respected and loved.

We arrived in Yokohama on a rainy night. Douglas caught a cold and was very depressed. I had never seen him so low before. The four-week voyage had been so wonderful that his unhappiness by contrast was devastating. I was afraid that perhaps he regretted our marriage, and told him so.

"No, my darling," he said, "it has nothing to do with you. I'm just not feeling well—I don't know why I feel so terrible." He pressed my hand. I found that he could tear himself down very easily. But I tried my best to bolster his spirits. As long as I wasn't the cause, I was willing to turn somersaults and stand on my head if it would make him happy.

To add to his grim mood, rain was pouring, the night was wet and cold, and the clamoring rickshaw men were fighting over who would take us to a hotel. Then I got drpressed too. I was wearing a mink coat; Douglas had on his Burberry raincoat. We were handed rice-paper parasols that miraculously kept the water off as we hopped into a rickshaw. It took a few minutes for us to get to the hotel. I became suddenly aware that our rickshaw, full of our hand luggage and us, was being pulled by two skinny, barefoot human beings running in unison like animals, and it made my stomach turn. I never got into a rickshaw again.

Yokohama was an overnight stop, with not terribly much to see, just the Japanese language and signs to get used to, and the sight of people in the streets who looked strangely small and doll-like. We left by train for Tokyo the next day. The weather had changed—it was sunny and bright, and so were Douglas's spirits. The train was clean, comfortable and fast. The food was good, and the Japanese landscape was gorgeous, terraced, manicured and divided like a patched quilt in colored squares for miles and miles. Every inch of the land was tilled. We pointed things out to each other like excited children. The Gestetners were with us. They were to be met by important business people in Tokyo and made plans to include us in the parties and entertainment planned for them. After Tokyo we were to go to Shanghai, and they to Singapore.

When we got off the train in Tokyo I had to go to the little girls' room. Douglas managed, with sign language, to find out which door I was to walk through. I told him I would see him in a few minutes, and walked through the door. To my astonishment I was in an enormous rectangular room with tile floor lined with holes on each side, and men and women doing their thing right in front of God and each other! I was so startled that I turned right around to run out when I saw Douglas walking in from the door next to the one I had walked through. I looked at him and blurted, "It's bad enough to see the strangers, but not you!" The experience froze my need until we got to the hotel.

We stayed at the famous Tokyo Kaikan designed by Frank Lloyd Wright after the Tokyo earthquake in 1908 and known all over the world as the Imperial Hotel. The Orient was much more "foreign" in the 1930's than today. For me Tokyo was a complete education, a new world before my eyes—the sparseness of decoration, the peace and serenity of the gardens and parks, the airy quality of the Shogi screens. The women looked like porcelain dolls, with their whitewashed faces, carefully painted red cupid mouths, slanted eyes and jet black lacquered elaborate haircombs that looked as if they were made out of something solid. I told Douglas that I couldn't imagine doing up one of those haircombs in less than three hours and wondered how they slept. I found out—on the floor on a mat—with one of those scooped-out oblong pillows that they rested their necks on. I still wonder how you can sleep all night without turning.

Douglas, whatever his moods, whatever his sense of guilt and regret over Lorraine and his languishing career, was determined that this honeymoon should be memorable for me. On our first evening in Tokyo we went with the Gestetners to an elegant restaurant, and on the next day, when our friends invited us to an inside look at Takashimaya, the gorgeous, enormous department store, Hennie and I ordered kimonos and hapi coats of pure silk, hand painted and embroidered, of soft and luscious colors, with our initials woven or printed into them. Douglas bought me two of each and I still have them.

Douglas was as astonished as I when we visited Mr. Mikimoto, known all over the world for his cultured pearls. Nobody else had copied his way of doing it, yet he was very old.

He showed us a string of pearls that had taken him forty years to cultivate. They were about 80 inches long, valued at $80,000. The next day we were taken to one of his farms, or hatcheries, and shown how they impregnated an oyster with a grain of sand, a very delicate process. We were told that there was no guarantee that the pearl would be perfect and round, or what color it would be. Some came out pink, gray, taupe, yellow, white, some round, others baroque, some pear-shaped. There were many beds for the oysters, each marked by the year it was started. We watched the girls sorting them and drilling for insertion of the thread so that in the end we could hang them around our necks.

Of course, Douglas wanted to buy me a string of pearls, and Sigmund wanted a string for Hennie. Mr. Mikimoto took us to the office, put out a tray and told us to choose. I was a little embarrassed, not knowing the price, and I whispered to Douglas that I didn't want to choose one too expensive. He asked Mr. Mikimoto how much the pearls were on one tray that held about fifteen strands. Mr. Mikimoto's eyes twinkled and he said, "The pearls on this tray are worth from $100 to $500 a strand—but whatever strands your ladies choose, they may have for $100. So whether you get a bargain depends on how much they learned about the quality of the pearls from our tour today." I was given on tray and Hennie another. It wasn't easy to choose. I picked out a medium, modest string, not because I thought it was the best but because it would be something Mrs. Douglas MacLean would wear with a simple black dress. Douglas approved of my choice, and after they were paid for, Mr. Mikimoto said that I had picked the most valuable strand on the tray.

The night before the Gestetners left to continue their journey, Sigmund gave a party in a geisha house. I believe that no Occidental woman had ever been invited to one before. It was a cool evening and I took my mink coat along; I made it into a mink rug, the only way I could sit on the floor. Hennie and I were the only women guests. Of the eight men besides our husbands, there were an Englishman, who represented the Gestetner office in Tokyo, and seven Japanese. They were polite and well educated; all spoke English, and were obviously men who had traveled the world. Six exquisite Geisha girls came out to dance, play, sing, help us with the food, and act as hostesses. They wore layered kimonos. They giggled and smiled, and after a beautiful dinner of elaborate variety, they motioned Hennie and me to follow them to what we call the powder room. The head girl, who looked absolutely unreal, wore a magnificent white, heavy silk brocade kimono with a gold obi. They wore the kimonos away from their necks, so around the collar it looked like layers of ombre ranging from the white top and went from pale pink to a brilliant red, the last line around the neck. I told Hennie I was curious about what they wore underneath, and said "Maybe we can make them understand." I pointed at her and at myself and pulled up my skirt to reveal the top of my stocking attached to a garter, and we both giggled. The geisha indicated she understood perfectly, and if I would take off my clothes, she would take off hers. Hennie was hysterical as the head geisha and I stood there stripping between the giggles and the laughter of the others. We counted the pieces we each took off—I had a dress, a slip, a bra, panties, and a garter belt, plus my stockings and shoes, which made a total of seven pieces. The geisha took off eight kimonos, each one a thinner silk of exquisite color: the last one crimson and very sheer. We counted the pieces, got dressed, and went back to join the men.

After the Gestetners left, Douglas and I were on our own. We continued our avid sightseeing and Douglas's worries disappeared as we toured. We went to Lake Hokoni, Mount Fuji, the perfect ice cream cone mountain that I had seen postcards of all my life. We stayed at a fascinating hotel run by an Englishman who claimed to have the longest moustache in the world. In that hotel I slept in a brass bed that had the down-feather perinas of my childhood instead of American mattresses. Douglas and I had two rooms. After getting one of the best massages I ever had for my aching muscles, I fell asleep in the perinas, just as I used to when I was a little girl in Russia.

Douglas didn't miss a museum, park, shrine, temple, or

antique shop. We saw every crook and cranny and I got the complete history of everything I saw. It was mind-boggling and fascinating. I don't know how much I absorbed, but I learned how much Douglas knew about comparative religion. I knew nothing about the religions of the world, but he had been interested in the subject all his life. Because his father was a minister and Douglas was a probing and curious man, he had taken to the subject, and questioned much about various interpretations of the Old and New Testaments. I heard phrases, names and words I never heard before: metaphysics, new-thought religion. He talked about Thoreau and Emerson and told me the story of Buddha. The last temple I remember in Japan was one big room at the top of a pyramid of lacquered steps. It seemed like a lot of steps, maybe equivalent to five stories. We were required to take off our shoes and put on a pair of slippers to climb to the top. When you reached the top, there seemed to be an open triangle. On each side of the triangle, approximately twice as large as life, were figures of every important religious figure—Mohammed, Buddha, Jesus, Moses, etc., and right in the center of the corner was a 30-foot gold circle, polished like a mirror, that was supposed to represent God. Of course, when you looked into it, you saw only your own reflection.

We left Japan with treasures I still have of lacquer bowls, Imari plates and bowls, drawings, etchings, kimonos and obis, and beautiful Japanese dolls made by hand of precious silk. In those days it was possible to take those things with you because we were traveling by ship and train, and we even had a crate of dishes with a complete service for twelve, and cooking ware for sukiyaki.

Douglas was a wonderful companion, particularly when he had an audience. His whole personality became instantly charged with charm and gaiety. He came alive and interested in anybody who remembered him. In the middle of the '30s there were many people all over the world who recognized him instantly from the almost 65 silent films that he starred in and produced.

I remember the rapid trip to Shanghai. It was a beautiful evening when we arrived in late September. We were met at the ship by Douglas's niece, Peggy Boyten, who had two men with her in the car to help us with our luggage and to take us to the most modern and fashionable hotel, The Park, facing the famous Shanghai race track. Waiting there in our suite of rooms—two bedrooms and a drawing room—was the amah, whom Peggy had hired for me. I am average height, about 5'4"—this little woman must have weighed eighty pounds, couldn't have been more than 4'10", had her hair pulled back severely in a bun, wore a black Chinese jacket and narrow blue pants. When I looked down at her feet, I was horrified; they were four-inch stubs. I couldn't see how she could walk on them. I had heard about bound feet, but I thought that they had gone out with the 19th century. Maybe it had, for I couldn't tell her age. Oriental faces don't seem to wrinkle and sag as much as ours do. Peggy explained that this woman would be my personal maid, do my hair, manicure, massage—anything or everything I thought of. I didn't really want her, and felt that having her around all day would affect my privacy, but I couldn't be impolite and didn't know exactly what Betty meant by "everything." When I found the amah asleep on the floor in front of my door the following morning, I found out what Peggy meant. She had got me a slave! I felt so guilty that I found all kinds of excuses to leave her in the hotel when I went shopping—although that was supposed to be one of her functions—because I felt that at least my amah could get some rest while I was out.

Shanghai was busy, mysterious and, of course, exciting. The first night we were taken to a fabulous casino, The Palace, that had a restaurant, gambling and whatever else you were looking for. I knew a few people who were living in Shanghai at that time—Rudolph Friml, the composer, with his Chinese wife, in a magnificent house, and J. P. McEvoy, who wrote the book for *Show Girl*, whom I had met at George Gershwin's when they were preparing the show. He too had a houseful of Chinese beauties who waited on him hand and foot. It was fascinating, and I was happy to introduce my husband to my talented, Bohemian and creative friends. Douglas had regained the composure he was so proud of. If he was still depressed, he didn't show it. We met more people and had a marvelous time. We met Mrs. Gray, who had an antique shop in Peking, and through her hospitality I saw the Great Wall. With her guidance and help Douglas let me buy three Kuan Yins of the Sung period, carved of wood, one of them sitting on a large elephant, that I cherish and still have. I never look at them without wishing I had known then what I know now about their value. I would have a million dollars worth of antiques, at least!

I met part of the Russian colony. They were a mixture of classes from old Russia, but they were all one class in China, mostly poor and desperate. I was able to speak their language a little. Cossacks who had to sell their silver, decorations, belts, buttons, and emblems from their uniforms and whatever else they had taken out of Russia. There were dance halls with Russian ladies of the night obviously trying to keep body and soul together. Many of the Russians were doormen, policemen, traffic cops, and waiters. A few smart ones made money. Most of the nobility had not been trained to make a living, and they were the most pathetic. A dinner was given for Douglas and me by General Tsean, who had been educated at Oxford and was the brother of the Soong sisters. The Chinese we met were cultivated, rich, brilliant and exquisite. I met some of the most beautiful Chinese women in the world, wearing native dress, a study in simplicity and grace, with beautiful jade and diamond jewelry worth a king's ransom.

The first day in China I tried to use chopsticks. I have never since eaten a Chinese meal any other way and I enjoy being accused of "showing off" but it actually tastes better that way. Douglas enjoyed seeing my eyes glow with excitement as I saw and discovered all these new wonders. Again I realized he was a born teacher. Life in Shanghai was varied and contradictory: the very rich with all the servants versus the opium dens, the prostitutes, and the very poor who lived on sampans in the smelly Yangtse River, some of them never leaving the boat. You could see the children and sometimes the old hanging over the side of the sampans while the mothers cooked dinner over a little open charcoal brazier at the other end. They were lucky if they got a piece of fish to supplement the endless rice diet that they were reduced to. The river was an open sewer but the same water was used to wash and cook the fish.

The Chinese theater and opera acted by young boys was fascinating but after seeing it a couple of times, and after two months of socializing, Douglas became restless. We didn't have a planned itinerary—he had said that we should stay in a town as long as we felt like it—and our next vague destination was to be Hong Kong and Singapore, but I could tell he was getting bored though I knew he didn't want to disappoint me. On the other hand, I realized that if he got depressed the trip would cease to be fun. So I asked him point blank to tell me if he had had enough. He was relieved and happy that I was ready to go home. We had been gone four months, and the trip back would take another month. It was the end of November and there was unrest in Shanghai. We made our plans and booked our passage back on a Canadian boat. We planned to be on the boat that New Year's Eve. The day we left, Shanghai was bombed by Japan, but we got out safely. We had been unaware of the tremendous danger.

Although the *Tatsuta-Maru* had been comfortable (they had even spoken English), the food was "universal," and we were happy to come over on it. Getting on a Canadian ship with people that looked like us and spoke our language was like coming home, and we settled down to a nice, long return. What we didn't count on was December on the high seas. It was lucky that Douglas was a yachtsman and that I had once traveled steerage. I would say that for half of the trip, most of the people in the staterooms were throwing up, and I'm sure that when we reached Honolulu we were all ten pounds thinner than when we started out.

But neither storm nor squall nor revolution nor Douglas's

occasional depressions nor even an earthquake could shake or mar my happiness. I considered myself the most fortunate of women that God had chosen me to stand on the landing in front of the elevator at the Playhouse on East 48th in 1932 to greet this man whom I had waited for all my life. Christmas on the boat was the third we had spent together and the first since we were married. With a jade ring and a half a dozen other thoughtful, surprising gifts, came this note:

Dearest: I am the most fortunate of men. Each Christmas I have the same gift. It is what I want most, need most. It brings me joy and happiness all through the year. Everyday I love to have it with me. It is my greatest blessing, my inspiration, my heart's desire. Your Douglas.

My throat filled with a lump; indeed I had been born in a lucky caul.

* * *

I surprised myself when I discovered that I had absolutely no qualms about giving up my acting career. True, I really didn't have much choice; it was either the theater in New York, or Douglas. I loved him, and he was the best possible man for me, Main-Line Philadelphia background, character, talent, charm, brains and manners. Although we came from different worlds this union was made in heaven and could only happen here in the country of my birth. Here a Barondess and MacLean could marry and live happily ever after.

I entered my thirties with a chance for a normal life with family and children. To add to my joy, my husband was a famous silent movie star, a writer, and now a producer. Our life style would be more than secure with a beautiful house in Beverly Hills, his 68-foot yacht *The Comrade* and we would travel all over the world living in comfort and style. I could develop my talents in the arts and maybe try to write.

Douglas had such beautiful taste and knew so much about

furniture, antiques, and architecture that it inspired me to learn about the things that interested him. His encouragement of everything I did and everything I wore was immensely flattering. I was sure that he was my God-sent prize, and I truly had achieved the American Dream. But all dreams come to an end when we awaken. Mine lasted for the best ten years of my life. I literally walked on air.

It will take another book to cover my next forty years. They were so full of the excitement of pursuit and fulfillment in areas I never dreamed possible. I suppose I achieved success, that's what they tell me, and I am grateful for the recognition and respect for my work and effort. The hits, runs, and errors taught me much about the art of survival—and how to start living "Another Life Another Time."